COOKWISE

A cookbook created for
Foundation Bariatric Affiliates'
WeightWise Bariatric Program

Chef Dave Fouts

Edited by: Jodie Gutkowski
Contributing editor: Dawn Atwater

Volume I

Foundation Bariatric *Affiliates*
14000 N. Portland Ave., Suite 202
Oklahoma City, Oklahoma 73134

Copyright © Foundation Bariatric *Affiliates* 2006

Manufactured in Canada by Friesens Corporation

Library of Congress Cataloging-in-Publication Data
Fouts, David
CookWise Volume 1/ by David Fouts

ISBN 0-9790500-5-7

Edited by: Jodie Gutkowski
Book design and art direction: Prism Publishing Center

First Printing November 2006

To my wife, **MARY**, who has given me the best ten years of my life, and to my two sons, **NOAH** and **MICHAEL**, who with their creative and sometimes funny minds demand that I strive higher.

To **DR. CYNTHIA BUFFINGTON**, who recognizes that obesity is a deadly disease and has made it her life's work to change the fate of others. And to everyone fighting the battle against obesity, both those who have won and those who are still fighting.

As mother always says, "you have to eat your veggies!" Although we don't always like to hear it, sometimes mother knows best. Proper nutrition is crucial for everyone, especially those involved in physical activity. Proper nutrition helps active people prevent injury, enhances recovery from exercise by building and repairing muscle fibers, achieves and maintains ideal body weight, improves daily workouts, and maintains overall health. Our bodies needs the proper amount of nutrients to sustain activity and to reach our goals whether they are weight loss, increase in muscle mass, weight gain, or competitive performance. Proper nutrition and optimal performance go hand in hand.

Somer Thompson
Exercise Physiologist
WeightWise Bariatric Program

Contents

Foreword

Finally, a real cookbook that we can recommend to our postsurgical and medical weight-loss patients!

Most diets, and hence most weight-loss programs, fall short because they fail to control hunger. Chef Dave has assembled recipes that are tasty (unusual in this category), are small in volume, and tend to control hunger. Several of the recipes involve pasta, which we do not condone for our surgical weight-loss patients, but the whole-wheat pasta does make sense for medical weight-loss patients and families of surgical weight-loss patients. That is, instead of making one recipe for the surgical weight-loss patient and one for the rest of the family, the "cook" can throw in some pasta and make a meal for the rest of the family or friends.

We can easily recommend Chef Dave based on his credentials. His classical culinary education, internships and executive chef record (in four-star restaurants) testify to his talent of crafting delicious fare. In addition to having culinary expertise, he is also a weight-loss surgery patient. This combination alone recommends him; however, his infectious personality and concern for food and people make him an invaluable asset to *our* overall weight-loss program . . . and this cookbook makes Chef Dave available for your program also.

Gregory F. Walton, MD, FACS
Chief of Bariatrics, Foundation Bariatric Hospital of Oklahoma
WeightWise Bariatric Program Surgeon

Preface

While dieting trends seem to change with the times, and methods of weight loss appear countless in number, there are key components to successful weight loss that transcend all diet trends and methods. These key components are behavior modification and permanent lifestyle changes. No matter what method of weight loss you have chosen, behavior modification and a commitment to a healthful way of life are necessary to ensure long-term weight-loss success. While easier said than done, a healthful way of life is less difficult if you have the right tools! CookWise is one of these tools. This collection of recipes can be used by a wide variety of individuals to create meals that are nutritious, are full of flavor, and can easily fit into a healthful lifestyle!

In particular, CookWise is a great tool for bariatric surgery patients. Among the countless weight-loss methods, bariatric surgery has become increasingly prevalent and has proven to be a very successful method for long-term weight-loss maintenance. As with other weight-loss programs, behavior modification and a healthful lifestyle are key to success after surgery. Behavior modifications may include, but are not limited to eating and drinking separately, taking small bites of food, chewing thoroughly, eating slowly, practicing conscious eating, and including protein-rich foods at each meal. While protein-rich foods are important after bariatric surgery, intolerances to beef or poultry are common. The combination of ingredients and preparation techniques found in these recipes allow bariatric surgery patients to eat and better tolerate those protein foods.

So whether or not you have had bariatric surgery, have yet to begin your weight-loss journey, or are on the road to success, CookWise can help you. Use this cookbook to incorporate individual recipes or various combinations of recipes into a nutritious way of life for your whole family. These recipes also provide a great opportunity to try new foods and expand your taste buds.

Remember, when you use the right tools, behavior modification and a commitment to a healthful lifestyle become less difficult. This will allow you to be successful in reaching your weight-loss goals!

Christina B. Corcoran, MS, RD/LD
Registered Dietitian
WeightWise Bariatric Program

APPETIZERS

*Never eat more
than you can lift.*
— **Miss Piggy**

Avocado Dip

The easiest guacamole you will ever make!

SERVINGS: 24

4 avocados, *cut in halves*
1 small red pepper, *diced*
1 bunch scallions, *diced*
½ bunch parsley, *diced fine*
¼ cup fresh lemon juice
1 teaspoon chili powder
2 cloves garlic, *diced fine*
1 teaspoon cumin
salt and pepper, *to taste*

First, place all ingredients in medium-size mixing bowl. Toss.

Then, place mixed ingredients into food processor. Blend until smooth.

Chill and serve.

NOTES: Add cilantro for a real Mexican flavor.

PER SERVING: 58 calories; 5 fat (73.9 calories from fat); 1 g protein; 3 g carbohydrate; 0 mg cholesterol; 6 mg sodium. Exchanges: 0 vegetable, 0 fruit, 0 lean meat, 1 fat.

SERVING IDEA:
Great used as a sandwich spread or vegetable dip.

Cheesy Apple-Stuffed Mushrooms

Mushrooms filled with apples and crumbled blue cheese; sweet and salty

SERVINGS: 32

32 large fresh mushrooms (*reserve ⅓ of stems*)
vegetable cooking spray
3 tablespoons celery, *finely chopped*
½ cup apple, *peeled and minced*
2 tablespoons dry, fine breadcrumbs
1 tablespoon fresh parsley, *chopped*
2 tablespoons walnuts, *finely chopped and toasted*
1 tablespoon crumbled blue cheese
2 teaspoons lemon juice
salt and pepper, *to taste*

SERVING IDEAS: Great as an appetizer or served as a side dish.

Clean mushrooms with damp paper towels. Remove stems. Reserve ⅓ of the mushroom stems, and chop fine.

Coat a small skillet with cooking spray; place over medium-high heat until hot.

Add ⅓ cup reserved chopped mushroom stems and celery; sauté 2 minutes or until tender.

Combine celery mix, apple, and next 7 ingredients in a small bowl, stir well.

Spoon 1½ teaspoons apple mix into each reserved mushroom cap.

Place mushrooms on a large pan. Bake at 350°F for 15 minutes.

NOTE: All ingredients need to be minced (chopped fine) in order to be stuffed into the mushrooms evenly.

PER SERVING: 11 calories; trace fat (32.0% calories from fat); 1 g protein; 2 g carbohydrate; trace dietary fiber; trace cholesterol; 9 mg sodium. Exchanges: 0 grain (starch); 0 lean meat; 0 vegetable; 0 fruit; 0 fat.

3

Chef Dave's Hummus

Simple and delicious

SERVINGS: 24

6 cups garbanzo beans, canned, *drained and rinsed*
¼ cup fresh lemon juice
¼ cup olive oil
2 teaspoons dried parsley
6 cloves garlic
¼ teaspoon cayenne
¼ cup tahini
salt and pepper, *to taste*

SERVING IDEA:
Great served with celery, carrot, or zucchini sticks.

Drain beans, and rinse with cold water.

Place all ingredients into food processor. Blend until smooth. Serve.

If dip is too thick, add more olive oil.

NOTE: Tahini is sesame seed paste and can be found in health food stores.

PER SERVING: 219 calories; 7 g fat (26.4% calories from fat); 10 g protein; 31 g carbohydrate; 9 g dietary fiber; 0 mg cholesterol; 15 mg sodium. Exchanges: 2 grain (starch); ½ lean meat; 0 vegetable; 0 fruit; 1 fat.

Garlic and Basil Bruschetta Dip

Fresh tomatoes tossed with garlic and fresh basil

SERVINGS: 12

2 large cloves garlic, *minced*
2 tablespoons extra virgin olive oil
1 teaspoon salt
½ teaspoon fresh ground black pepper
4 large tomatoes, *chopped*
½ bunch fresh basil leaves, *chopped*

Place all ingredients into a large bowl, and toss lightly.

Place in refrigerator for 2 hours. Serve

NOTE: The longer this marinates in its own juices, the better it is. I make this in the morning to have in the evening with dinner.

PER SERVING: 29 calories; 2 g fat (68.1% calories from fat); trace protein; 2 g carbohydrate; trace dietary fiber; 0 mg cholesterol; 181 mg sodium. Exchanges: 0 grain (starch); ½ vegetable; ½ fat.

SERVING IDEAS:
This is great over grilled chicken or fish, or used as topping on toasted French bread.

Simple Salsa

A simple, can't-go-wrong salsa

SERVINGS: 4

2 large tomatoes
¼ large jalapeño, *seeded and chopped*
3 cloves garlic
2 tablespoons lime juice
¼ bunch cilantro
½ small onion
1 teaspoon salt
1 teaspoon cumin

SERVING IDEAS:
Place over chicken, seafood, fish, beef, pork, or any other dish to spice it up.

Place tomatoes, jalapeño, garlic, lime juice, cilantro, onion, salt and cumin into food processor, and puree for 30 to 45 seconds.

NOTE: The less you puree, the chunkier it will be.

PER SERVING: 26 calories; trace fat (10.6% calories from fat); 1 g protein; 6 g carbohydrate; 1 g dietary fiber; 0 mg cholesterol; 540 mg sodium. Exchanges: 0 grain (starch); 0 lean meat; 1 vegetable; 0 fruit; 0 fat.

Smoky Scallops

Large scallops wrapped in bacon and basted with barbecue sauce

SERVINGS: 24

> 24 large scallops
> 1 pound bacon slices, *cut in 3-inch pieces*
> ½ cup barbecue sauce
> cracked black pepper, *to taste*
> toothpicks

SERVING IDEAS:
Great as a meal or as a delicious appetizer.

Wrap each scallop with a piece of bacon.

Using a long toothpick secure bacon scallop. Using a pastry brush, baste bacon wrapped scallops with BBQ sauce until whole piece is coated.

Place on grill over medium coals, or place in oven at 350°F. Cook for 15 minutes or until scallops are desired temperature.

Serve.

NOTE: If scallop is too big for bacon slice, cut scallop in half.

PER SERVING: 67 calories; 5 g fat (66.0% calories from fat); 5 g protein; 1 g carbohydrate; trace dietary fiber; 11 mg cholesterol, 209 mg sodium. Exchanges: ½ lean meat; ½ fat; 0 other carbohydrates.

Spicy Gorgonzola Cheese–Stuffed Eggs

Spicy deviled eggs

SERVINGS: 24

12 eggs, *hard boiled*
½ cup gorgonzola cheese, *crumbled*
¼ cup light mayonnaise
1 teaspoon fresh lemon juice
½ teaspoon Tabasco sauce
½ teaspoon salt
¼ teaspoon pepper
½ teaspoon celery salt
1 tablespoon parsley, *minced*

SERVING IDEAS: Perfect for any get-together or as a picnic side dish.

Hard boil eggs. Cool.

Next, shell eggs, and then cut them in half to make 24 egg halves.

Mash the yolks, and mix well with all other ingredients.

Finally, spoon the mixture into hollowed egg halves.

NOTE: Eggs are easy to peel while they are warm.

PER SERVING: 61 calories; 5 g fat (67.0% calories from fat); 4 g protein; 1 g carbohydrate; trace dietary fiber; 111 mg cholesterol; 194 mg sodium. Exchanges: 0 grain (starch); ½ lean meat; 0 vegetable; 0 fruit; ½ fat; 0 other carbohydrates.

Strawberry and Mango Salsa

A spicy fruit salsa

SERVINGS: 10

> 1 pint strawberries, *stems removed and washed*
> 1 large mango, *peeled, seeded and chopped*
> ¼ cup lime juice
> ½ cup onion, *peeled and chopped*
> ¼ bunch cilantro, *chopped*
> 1 clove garlic
> ½ jalapeño, *seeded*
> salt and pepper, *to taste*

Place all ingredients into food processor, and blend until desired consistency.

Chill and serve.

NOTE: For desired spiciness, add less or more jalapeño.

PER SERVING: 28 calories; trace fat (5.1% calories from fat); trace protein; 7 g carbohydrate; 1 g dietary fiber; 0 mg cholesterol; 1 mg sodium. Exchanges: 0 grain (starch); 0 lean meat; 0 vegetable; ½ fruit; 0 fat.

SERVING IDEAS:
Great served with chicken, fish, or seafood.

Surf and Turf Kabobs

Seasoned steak and shrimp placed on a wooden skewer and grilled

SERVINGS: 24

48 medium shrimp, *peeled and deveined*
1½ pounds beef tenderloin, *cut into 24 1-inch cubes*
2 teaspoons granulated garlic
1 teaspoon salt
1 teaspoon black pepper
1 teaspoon onion powder
1 teaspoon chili powder
1 teaspoon thyme
2 tablespoons olive oil
24 wooden skewers, *4-inch*

SERVING IDEA:
Great with horseradish sauce.

In a large mixing bowl combine all food ingredients, and mix well.

Let marinate 30 minutes to overnight.

Next, place 2 shrimp and 1 beef cube onto each skewer.

Then, place skewers over medium coals on grill; cook for 7 minutes or until shrimp is fully cooked.

Serve.

NOTE: You can also bake at 350°F or sauté over medium-high heat.

PER SERVING: 105 calories; 8 g fat (68.8% calories from fat); 8 g protein; trace carbohydrate; trace dietary fiber; 38 mg cholesterol; 121 mg sodium. Exchanges: 0 grain (starch); 1 lean meat; 1 fat.

Teriyaki Beef Sticks

Marinated beef tenderloin skewered and sautéed

SERVINGS: 16

1 pound beef tenderloin, *cut into 3-inch thin strips*
½ cup teriyaki sauce
½ bunch scallions, *chopped*
1 tablespoon garlic powder
1 tablespoon sesame oil
1 teaspoon crushed red pepper
¼ teaspoon olive oil
16 wooden skewers, *4-inch*

SERVING IDEA:
Garnish with chopped parsley and fresh grated ginger.

Place all ingredients into a medium mixing bowl, and marinate for 1 hour in refrigerator.

Once done marinating, divide meat evenly, and place onto skewers.

In a large skillet on medium-high heat, add olive oil.

Once olive oil is hot, add skewered meat, and sauté for 1 minute on each side.

Serve.

PER SERVING: 98 calories; 7 g fat (69.0% calories from fat); 6 g protein; 2 g carbohydrate; trace dietary fiber; 20 mg cholesterol; 359 mg sodium. Exchanges: 0 grain (starch), 1 lean meat, ½ vegetable, 1 fat.

BEEF

The only time to eat diet food is while you are waiting for the steak to cook.

—Julia Child

Beef Bourguignon

This is one of my all-time favorite dishes and well worth the wait.

SERVINGS: 12

2 teaspoons vegetable oil
½ pound fresh mushrooms, *cleaned and sliced*
3 small onions, *sliced*
1 pound boneless beef chuck, *cut into 1-inch pieces*
1 teaspoon salt
⅛ teaspoon pepper ¼ teaspoon thyme
¼ teaspoon oregano 1½ tablespoons flour
¾ cup beef broth 1½ cups Burgundy wine

SERVING IDEA:
Great served
on top of wild rice.

In a large skillet, brown mushrooms and onions in preheated oil. Cook and stir until onions are tender; remove vegetables, and set aside.

Brown meat in same skillet; remove from heat.

Add the salt, pepper, thyme, oregano and flour; mix well.

Stir in the beef broth, return to heat, and bring to a boil, stirring constantly.

Boil for 1 minute, stir in the Burgundy. Cover, and simmer for 1½ to 2 hours or until meat is tender. If necessary, add ⅓ cup broth and ⅔ cups wine to ensure that the broth always covers the meat.

Stir in the cooked onions and mushrooms, and cook uncovered for 15 minutes or until heated through.

NOTES: Pork can be used instead of beef. This dish freezes very well.

PER SERVING: 129 calories; 7 g fat (55.6% calories from fat); 7 g protein; 5 g carbohydrate; 1 g dietary fiber; 22 mg cholesterol; 297 mg sodium. Exchanges: 0 grain (starch); 1 lean meat; ½ vegetable; 1 fat.

Beef Tenderloin

*Beef tenderloin rubbed with herbs and olive oil
and roasted to perfection*

SERVINGS: 15

    1 whole beef tenderloin, *trimmed*
    3 tablespoons dried thyme
    3 tablespoons dried basil
    3 tablespoons dried oregano
    3 tablespoons granulated garlic
    ¼ cup olive oil
    2 tablespoons salt
    2 tablespoons cracked black pepper

Place all ingredients except beef into food processor, and blend well.

Spread herb mix over beef tenderloin.

Roast at 375°F until internal temperature is 145°F (medium).

NOTE: To save time, have your butcher prepare and tie the beef tenderloin while at the
grocery store.

PER SERVING: 90 calories; 7 g fat (70.7% calories from fat); 3 g protein; 3 g carbohydrate;
       1 g dietary fiber; 11 mg cholesterol; 862 mg sodium. Exchanges: 0 grain (starch);
       ½ lean meat; 1 fat.

Cheddar–Beef Philly Wrap

Melt-in-your-mouth cheesy roast beef

SERVINGS: 10

1 pound beef top round, *sliced thin (shaved)*
1 large white onion, *sliced*
10 slices low-fat cheddar cheese
1 teaspoon garlic powder
1 teaspoon onion powder
1 teaspoon olive oil
10 flour tortillas, whole wheat

SERVING IDEA:
Serve with baby
greens salad.

Horseradish sauce

1 teaspoon horseradish
1 tablespoon light mayonnaise
1 tablespoon light sour cream
1 clove garlic, *chopped fine*

To a large sauté pan over medium heat, add olive oil. Once olive oil is hot, add meat, onions and seasonings. Sauté for 2 minutes, and remove from stove.

To make the sauce, combine horseradish, mayonnaise, sour cream and garlic. Mix well.

Spread horseradish sauce over the tortillas, and divide meat mixture evenly over the tortillas. Next, place 1 slice of cheese over the top of each meat-filled tortilla.

Roll tortilla. Serve.

PER SERVING: 284 calories; 10 g fat (32.6% calories from fat); 21 g protein; 26 g carbohydrate; 2 g dietary fiber; 34 mg cholesterol; 412 mg sodium. Exchanges: 1½ grain (starch); 2½ lean meat; 0 vegetable; ½ fat; 0 other carbohydrates.

Corned Beef and Cabbage

The perfect one-pot meal with all the trimmings

SERVINGS: 16

1 large corn beef brisket, *already seasoned*
2 cabbage heads, *cut-up*
1 pound baby carrots
2 pounds red potatoes, *leave whole*
1 teaspoon celery seed
1 large onion, *sliced*
2 cloves garlic, *minced*
2 bay leaves
salt and pepper, *to taste*

SERVING IDEA:
Garnish with fresh parsley.

Oven

Set the oven for 350°F or no lower than 325°F. Place brisket fat side up, all root vegetables, cabbage and spices into a large roasting pan. Barely cover the meat with water—about 1 inch—and keep the container covered throughout the cooking time. Allow about 1 hour per pound.

Slow Cooker

If using root vegetables, put them in the bottom of the slow cooker. Cut brisket into pieces of like size to ensure thorough cooking. Place brisket on top of vegetables (if using) or in bottom of cooker. Add about 1½ cups of water or enough to cover meat. Cover and cook on high setting for the first hour of cooking. Then cook for 10 to 12 hours on the low setting, or 5 to 6 hours on high. Cabbage wedges may be added on top of the brisket during the last 3 hours of cooking.

NOTE: When preparing the corn beef, do not rinse, and add the seasoning packet that comes with the brisket.

PER SERVING: 154 calories; 1 g fat (4.3% calories from fat); 6 g protein; 34 g carbohydrate; 7 g dietary fiber; 0 mg cholesterol; 49 mg sodium. Exchanges: 1 grain (starch); 0 lean meat; 2½ vegetable; 0 fat.

Just-Right Chili

Chili with all the flavor, but not all the heat

SERVINGS: 8

½ pound lean beef, *ground*
½ pound lean pork, *ground*
2 teaspoons garlic, *chopped*
½ bunch scallions, *chopped*
14 ounces tomato sauce
14 ounces diced tomatoes, *drained*
2 teaspoons chili powder
1 teaspoon cumin
½ teaspoon black pepper
1 can pinto beans, *drained and rinsed*

Place ground beef and pork into a medium pot, and sauté for 5 minutes.

Drain fat.

Add remaining ingredients, and bring to a simmer.

Let simmer for 20 minutes.

Serve.

PER SERVING: 187 calories; 7 g fat (30.7% calories from fat); 11 g protein; 22 g carbohydrate; 7 g dietary fiber; 21 mg cholesterol; 334 mg sodium. Exchanges: 1 grain (starch); 1 lean meat; 1 vegetable; 1 fat.

Rib-Eye Pinwheel

Rib-eye steak stuffed with basil and sautéed

SERVINGS: 8

1 pound beef rib eye, *sliced ¼ inch thick*
1 bunch fresh basil, *chopped*
2 teaspoons Italian seasoning
2 teaspoons garlic powder
½ teaspoon chili powder
½ teaspoon black pepper
1 tablespoon Worcestershire sauce

2 tablespoons olive oil
2 teaspoons onion powder
½ teaspoon celery seed
1 teaspoon salt

SERVING IDEA:
Serve with
Death-by-Garlic
Sauce.

Pound out each steak to ¼ inch thick.

Next, place all ingredients except basil and 1 tablespoon olive oil into a small mixing bowl, and mix well. This is your paste.

Lay out the pounded rib eye, and spread herbed paste over one side. (Remember to reserve enough paste for all the steaks.)

Add fresh basil. (Remember to reserve enough basil for all the steaks.)

Next, roll steak tightly, using butcher's string to tie rolled steak to keep it from opening.

Over medium-high heat, add reserved olive oil to pan. Once oil is hot, add the rolled steak to pan, and sauté on all sides, turning frequently.

Sauté for 7 to 8 minutes. Let steak rest for 2 minutes. Slice steak into ½-inch pinwheels. Serve.

NOTE: Ask your butcher to slice the rib eye. Also, these steaks can be grilled over medium heat.

PER SERVING: 167 calories; 13 g fat (72.1% calories from fat); 10 g protein; 2 g carbohydrate; trace dietary fiber; 37 mg cholesterol; 318 mg sodium. Exchanges: 0 grain (starch); 1½ lean meat; 0 vegetable; 1½ fat; 0 other carbohydrates.

Rum-Marinated Rib-Eye Steaks

Steaks marinated with oregano, rum and garlic

SERVINGS: 4

1 pound rib-eye steaks, (New York strip),
  cut into 4-ounce steaks

Marinade

½ cup rum
¼ cup olive oil
1 tablespoon chili powder
2 large cloves garlic, *chopped*
1 teaspoon oregano
¼ teaspoon hot sauce

SERVING IDEA:
Garnish with
chopped parsley.

Place steak and all ingredients into a large self-sealing plastic bag.

Marinate steaks for 30 minutes to 2 hours. Remove steaks, and discard marinade.

Sauté in a large pan over medium-high heat for 5 to 8 minutes, turning every 2 minutes.

Serve.

NOTES: These steaks are great cooked on a grill. Pork can be substituted.

PER SERVING: 74 calories; 3 g fat (27.4% calories from fat); 19 g protein; 2 g carbohydrate;
1 g dietary fiber; 14 mg cholesterol; 27 mg sodium. Exchanges: 0 grain (starch);
2½ lean meat; 0 vegetable; 1 fat.

Sesame Beef with Garlic Goat Cheese

Beef sautéed and smothered with cheese

SERVINGS: 8

1½ pounds beef tenderloin, *cut into 4-ounce steaks*
½ teaspoon sesame oil
salt and pepper, *to taste*

Garlic Goat Cheese

1 clove garlic, *finely chopped*
1 ounce light cream cheese, *cut into cubes*
1 ounce goat cheese
2 tablespoons fresh parsley, *chopped fine*
½ teaspoon cracked black pepper

SERVING IDEA:
Garnish with chopped scallions.

Place beef into medium mixing bowl, and add sesame oil, salt and pepper. Mix well.

Heat large sauté pan. Once pan is hot, add beef tenderloin, and sauté for 2 minutes on each side. Remove from pan.

To make garlic goat cheese, combine cream cheese, garlic, goat cheese, parsley and pepper in a large mixing bowl, and mix well.

Next, divide cheese mixture evenly over the top of the steaks.

Place under broiler, and melt cheese.

Serve.

NOTE: This is also a great dish for the grill.

PER SERVING: 268 calories; 22 fat (74.1% calories from fat); 17 g protein; trace carbohydrate; trace dietary fiber; 66 mg cholesterol; 74 mg sodium. Exchanges: 0 grain (starch); 2 lean meat; 0 vegetables; 3 fat; 0 other carbohydrates.

Stir-Fried Beef and Spinach with Noodles

Tasty, easy-to-make, warm Asian salad

SERVINGS: 12

1 pound beef rib eye, *¼ inch thick*
16-ounce package whole-wheat pasta
1 10-ounce package fresh spinach, *stems removed*
1 8-ounce can sliced water chestnuts, *drained*
¼ cup green onion, *sliced*
½ teaspoon red chili peppers, *chopped* (optional)

SERVING IDEA:
Garnish with
chili peppers.

Marinade

¼ cup hoisin sauce
1 tablespoon water
2 large cloves garlic, *crushed*

2 tablespoons soy sauce
1 teaspoon sesame oil
¼ teaspoon red pepper *crushed* (optional)

Combine marinade ingredients, and pour half over beef. Cover, and marinate in refrigerator for 10 minutes. Reserve remaining marinade.

Meanwhile, cook pasta according to package directions; keep warm.

Remove beef from marinade; discard used marinade.

Heat large nonstick wok or skillet over medium-high heat until hot.

Add beef (half at a time) and stir-fry 2 minutes. Remove from skillet with slotted spoon; keep warm.

In same skillet, combine pasta, spinach, water chestnuts, green onions and reserved marinade; cook until spinach is wilted and mixture is heated through, stirring occasionally.

Return beef to skillet; mix lightly. Serve.

PER SERVING: 182 calories; 9 g fat (43.0% calories from fat); 10 g protein; 17 g carbohydrate; 3 g dietary fiber; 25 mg cholesterol; 300 mg sodium. Exchanges: ½ grain (starch); 1 lean meat; ½ vegetable; 1 fat; 0 other carbohydrates.

Stuffed Herbed Beef Tenderloin

Beef tenderloin stuffed with herbs and Asiago cheese

SERVINGS: 6

1 pound beef tenderloin, *butterflied and pounded thin*
1 teaspoon thyme, *chopped* — 2 cloves garlic, *minced*
1 teaspoon basil, *whole leaves* — ¼ cup red wine
1 teaspoon oregano, *chopped* — ½ cup Asiago cheese, *grated*
3 tablespoons olive oil — salt and pepper, *to taste*
½ teaspoon red pepper flakes
1 teaspoon Worcestershire sauce

SERVING IDEA:
Garnish with
fresh chopped basil.

Pound the butterflied beef thin. Rub minced garlic, thyme, basil, oregano, red pepper flakes, Worcestershire sauce and 1 tablespoon olive oil over the top of the filet.

Add cheese over seasoned meat.

Next, starting at one end of the meat, roll tightly. Using butcher twine, tie filet to keep it rolled together.

Finally, in a large skillet add remaining olive oil, and sauté meat over medium heat, turning every 5 minutes for 30 minutes (cooking time will vary depending on how you like your beef cooked). Remove meat from skillet, and deglaze pan with red wine. Place stuffed filet on a serving dish, and pour red wine over meat. Serve.

NOTES: The meat can also be baked in the oven at 350°F for 35 minutes or longer if you like it more well done. Also, have your butcher prepare the raw beef tenderloin for this dish; this will save you time in the kitchen.

PER SERVING: 243 calories; 19 g fat (72.7% calories from fat); 15 g protein; 1 g carbohydrate; trace dietary fiber; 59 mg cholesterol; 87 mg sodium. Exchanges: 0 grain (starch); 3 lean meat; 0 vegetable; 4 fat; 0 other carbohydrates.

Swedish Meatballs

Beef meatballs with sour cream sauce

SERVINGS: 8

1 pound fresh ground beef
1 large egg
1 teaspoon basil
1 teaspoon thyme
1 teaspoon onion powder

¼ cup Parmesan cheese
1 teaspoon oregano
1 teaspoon garlic powder

Sauce

1 cup light sour cream
½ cup skim milk
1 tablespoon beef bouillon granules
1 teaspoon garlic powder
salt and pepper, *to taste*

SERVING IDEAS:
Garnish with fresh chopped basil. Also great with cottage cheese.

In a large mixing bowl, combine ground beef, egg, Parmesan cheese, basil, oregano, thyme, garlic powder and onion powder.

Next, roll meatball mixture into 2-inch round balls with your hands.

Bake at 350°F for 20 minutes. Remove from oven, and set aside.

In a medium pot, combine sour cream, skim milk, beef bouillon granules, garlic powder, salt and pepper over medium heat.

Stir constantly until mixture begins to lightly simmer. Add meatballs, and let simmer on low for 5 minutes. Serve.

NOTE: It is very important to stir the sour cream sauce constantly and not let it come to a boil to prevent the sauce from burning and separating.

PER SERVING: 192 calories; 14 g fat (65.2% calories from fat); 13 g protein; 3 g carbohydrate; trace dietary fiber; 74 mg cholesterol; 237 mg sodium. Exchanges: 0 grain (starch); 2 lean meat; 0 nonfat milk; 1½ fat; 0 other carbohydrates.

Tequila Green Peppercorn Filet Tips

Beef tenderloin tips smothered in a tequila
and green peppercorn sauce

SERVINGS: 4

1 pound beef top round, *cut into ½-inch pieces*
2 tablespoons olive oil
1 clove garlic, *crushed*
1 teaspoon onion powder
1 teaspoon rosemary, *chopped fine*
1 teaspoon salt
2 tablespoons green peppercorns
1 ounce tequila
1 tablespoon Worcestershire sauce
¼ cup light cream cheese
¼ cup beef stock (used to thin out the sauce if too thick)

SERVING IDEA:
Garnish with whole fresh basil leaves.

To a large sauté pan over medium-high heat, add olive oil.

Once olive oil is hot, add beef tips, garlic, onion powder, rosemary, salt and green peppercorns, and sauté beef for 3 minutes.

Add tequila to deglaze pan.

Stir in Worcestershire sauce, cream cheese, and, if needed, add beef stock.

Bring to a light simmer, then remove from heat. Serve.

NOTE: Chicken or pork can be substituted for beef (cook time will increase).

PER SERVING: 226 calories; 13 g fat (56.2% calories from fat); 18 g protein; 6 g carbohydrate; 2 g dietary fiber; 51 mg cholesterol; 562 mg sodium. Exchanges: ½ grain (starch); 2½ lean meat; 0 vegetable; 1 fat; 0 other carbohydrates.

Teriyaki Portobello Beef

Beef tenderloin sautéed with portobello mushrooms and bean sprouts

SERVINGS: 6

1 pound beef skirt steak, *sliced into thin, short strips*
1 teaspoon peanut oil
2 cloves garlic, *chopped*
2 cups portobello mushrooms, *sliced thin*
2 cups bean sprouts
1 cup scallions, *chopped*
1 teaspoon ground ginger
¼ cup teriyaki sauce
½ teaspoon sesame oil
salt and pepper, *to taste*

SERVING IDEAS:
Great over
lo mein noodles
or fried rice.

To a large sauté pan over medium-high heat, add peanut oil. Once oil is hot, add beef and garlic, and sauté for 2 minutes.

Next, add mushrooms, bean sprouts, scallions and ground ginger, and sauté for 5 minutes.

Add teriyaki sauce, sesame oil, salt and pepper, and sauté for 2 minutes.

Serve.

NOTE: Great with chicken and pork also.

PER SERVING: 138 calories; 7 g fat (44.7% calories from fat); 13 g protein; 6 g carbohydrate; 1 g dietary fiber; 29 mg cholesterol; 390 mg sodium. Exchanges: 0 grain (starch); 1½ lean meat; 1 vegetable; ½ fat.

BREAKFAST

*My wife and I tried
to breakfast together,
but we had to stop or our marriage
would have been wrecked.*

—**Winston Churchill**

Chef Dave's Crepe Cheese Filling

Ricotta cheese and spices create a smooth and tasty cheese filling

SERVINGS: 16

8 ounces ricotta cheese, *part skim milk*
8 ounces light cream cheese, *softened*
½ teaspoon vanilla extract
¼ teaspoon nutmeg
¼ teaspoon cinnamon
¼ cup Splenda

SERVING IDEA:
This is a perfect filling for Low-Fat Honey Crepes.

Place all ingredients into a large mixing bowl, and mix for 2 minutes or until mixture is smooth.

PER SERVING: 53 calories; 4 fat (62.4% calories from fat); 3 protein; 2 carbohydrate; trace dietary fiber; 12 cholesterol; 97 sodium. Exchanges: 0 grain (starch); ½ lean meat; ½ fat; 0 other carbohydrates.

Low-Fat Honey Crepes

Light egg batter transformed into a light airy pancake
and stuffed with salads, fruits and meats.

SERVINGS: 4

    2 cups nonfat milk
    1 cup all-purpose flour
    2 egg whites
    1 egg
    1 tablespoon honey
    1 tablespoon vegetable oil
    ⅛ teaspoon salt

SERVING IDEAS:
Fill with ricotta
cheese filling and/or
fresh sliced fruit.

Combine all ingredients in a blender or food processor; blend until smooth.

Rub an 8-inch nonstick skillet with an oiled paper towel, or spray lightly with nonstick cooking spray; heat over medium-high heat.

Spoon 3 to 4 tablespoons crepe batter into skillet, tilting and rotating skillet to cover evenly with batter.

Cook until edges begin to brown. Turn crepe over, and cook until lightly browned.

Remove crepe to plate to cool. Repeat process with remaining batter.

PER SERVING: 57 calories; 1 g fat (20.5% calories from fat); 3 g protein; 9 g carbohydrate; trace dietary fiber; 14 mg cholesterol; 44 mg sodium. Exchanges: ½ grain (starch); 0 lean meat; 0 nonfat milk; 0 fat; 0 other carbohydrates.

Mojo Chicken Omelet

Marinated chicken stuffed in a cheesy omelet

SERVINGS: 4

8 large eggs
2 tablespoons skim milk
1 cup boneless, skinless chicken breast, *½-inch cubes*
¾ cup mojo marinade (found in your local grocery store)
4 teaspoons butter
2 teaspoons fresh chives, *chopped*
salt and pepper, *to taste*

1 teaspoon garlic, *chopped*
2 teaspoons fresh cilantro, *chopped*
1 cup cheese, *shredded*

SERVING IDEA:
Garnish with fresh cilantro and light sour cream.

Marinate chicken in mojo marinade for 1 hour.

In a large mixing bowl, combine eggs and skim milk, and mix well.

Next, in an 8-inch sauté pan over medium heat, place 1 teaspoon butter, and melt.

Add ¼ teaspoon garlic, ½ teaspoon chives, ½ teaspoon cilantro, ¼ cup of chicken, and sauté for 6 minutes.

Pour ¼ of egg mixture over sautéed chicken. Egg will begin to firm up. Once egg is firm enough, use a spatula to flip.

Add ¼ cup of cheese on top of cooked egg, and fold ½ of cooked egg over top. Salt and pepper to taste. Serve hot.

Repeat process for the remaining omelets.

NOTES: Always use a Teflon-coated pan to keep omelet from sticking. Mojo is a Spanish marinade and can be purchased at your local grocery store, or you can make it. See recipe in Salad Dressings and Sauces.

PER SERVING: 251 calories; 15 g fat (53.8% calories from fat); 27 g protein; 1 g carbohydrate; trace dietary fiber; 469 mg cholesterol; 222 mg sodium. Exchanges: 3½ lean meat; 0 vegetable; 0 nonfat milk; 1½ fat.

Sausage Spanish Omelet

Eggs stuffed with veggies, sausage and cheese

SERVINGS: 1

2 large eggs
1 tablespoon water
cooking spray
1 ounce ground sausage, *cooked*
1 teaspoon bell pepper, *chopped*
1 teaspoon onion, *chopped*
1 teaspoon tomato, *chopped*
2 teaspoons cheddar cheese, low-fat, *shredded*

SERVING IDEAS:
Garnish with
a salsa. See Simple
Salsa recipe.

For each omelet, beat together 2 large eggs and 1 tablespoon of water.

Spray a 7- to 10-inch omelet pan or skillet with cooking spray, and set over medium heat.

Add bell pepper, onions and tomatoes. Sauté vegetables for 2 minutes.

Next, pour in egg mixture. Mixture should be set immediately to edges.

With an inverted spatula, carefully push cooked portions at edges toward center so uncooked portions can reach hot pan surface. While drawing cooked portions toward center, tilt pan, and move cooked portions as necessary.

While top is still moist and creamy looking, add sausage and cheese on one side of omelet.

With spatula fold unfilled side of omelet over filling. Do not worry if it tears. When flipped onto a plate, tears will not be visible. Serve.

NOTE: Always use a Teflon-coated pan to keep omelet from sticking.

PER SERVING: 159 calories; 10 g fat (60.1% calories from fat); 14 g protein; 2 g carbohydrate; trace
dietary fiber; 425 mg cholesterol; 170 mg sodium. Exchanges: 2 lean meat; 0 vegetable;
1 fat.

Ultimate Breakfast Wrap

Whole-wheat tortilla filled with eggs, cheese and sausage

SERVINGS: 2

2 whole-wheat flour tortillas
2 large eggs
1 ounce sausage (ground), *cooked*
2 tablespoons green bell pepper, *diced*
2 tablespoons onion, *diced*
2 tablespoons tomatoes, *diced*
2 tablespoons Monterey pepper jack cheese, *grated*
salt and pepper, *to taste*

SERVING IDEAS:
Top with salsa and
light sour cream.

Warm tortilla.

Spray a 7- to 10-inch skillet with cooking spray, and place over medium heat.

Next, add bell pepper, onion and tomatoes, and sauté for 2 minutes.

Add eggs and sausage, and scramble until eggs are soft and fluffy.

Fill tortilla with half the egg mixture and half the cheese.

Fold and close wrap. Serve.

Repeat for second tortilla.

PER SERVING: 309 calories; 8 g fat (25.1% calories from fat); 12 g protein; 45 g carbohydrate; 3 g dietary fiber; 108 mg cholesterol; 422 mg sodium. Exchanges: 3 grain (starch); ½ lean meat; ½ vegetable; 1 fat.

Yogurt and Berry Crepe Blintzes

Crepes smothered in yogurt and fresh berries

SERVINGS: 8

8 prepared crepes
1½ cups low-fat cottage cheese
3 ounces Neufchâtel cheese (found in your grocer's
   specialty-cheese dairy case)

⅓ cup sugar substitute	1 teaspoon vanilla
1 tablespoon fresh-squeezed lemon juice	½ teaspoon lemon zest
	1 tablespoon vegetable oil

SERVING IDEA:
Top with fresh berries and a mint leaf for garnish.

Yogurt Berry Sauce

1 cup nonfat plain yogurt	2 cups fresh strawberries, *sliced*
1 cup fresh raspberries	1 cup fresh blueberries

½ teaspoon lemon extract (do not use lemon juice;
   this will make the yogurt curdle)
⅓ cup sugar substitute

Mix together cottage cheese, Neufchâtel cheese, sugar substitute, vanilla, lemon juice and zest.

Fill each crepe. Fold.

Next, in a medium sauté pan, preheat oil, and slightly brown stuffed crepes.

To make sauce, combine yogurt, berries, lemon extract and sugar substitute in a medium mixing bowl.

Mix lightly, and refrigerate until needed.

Place yogurt berry sauce over crepes while still warm. Serve.

NOTE: Any fresh fruit can be used.

PER SERVING: 142 calories; 2 g fat (15.6% calories from fat); 7 g protein; 23 g carbohydrate; 3 g dietary fiber; 2 mg cholesterol; 211 mg sodium. Exchanges: ½ lean meat; ½ fruit; 0 nonfat milk; ½ fat; 1 other carbohydrates.

FISH AND SEAFOOD

*Why does Sea World have
a seafood restaurant? I'm halfway
through my fish burger and I realize,
Oh my God . . . I could be eating
a slow learner.*

—Lyndon B. Johnson

Champagne-Poached Salmon

Salmon poached in sweet champagne, capers and lime

SERVINGS: 4

4 4-ounce salmon steaks, *skinned and boned*
2 cups champagne
¼ cup fresh lime juice
4 slices red onion
1 tablespoon capers, *optional*
4 sprigs fresh tarragon
½ cup honey Dijon mustard
1½ teaspoons fresh tarragon, *chopped*
salt and pepper, *to taste*

> **SERVING IDEA:**
> Great with
> Strawberry and
> Mango Salsa.

Mix together mustard and chopped tarragon; set aside.

Season salmon steaks lightly with salt and pepper.

Place in a pan just large enough to hold the salmon in 1 layer. Add the champagne, lime juice, and just enough water to cover the fish.

Remove the fish, and bring the liquid to a boil.

Return the fish to the pan.

Top each with an onion slice, capers and tarragon sprig.

Reduce heat to a simmer, cover pan with foil, and poach at no more than a simmer for 6 to 10 minutes (depending on the thickness of the salmon).

Remove salmon steaks or fillets from the liquid and place on 4 warm serving plates.

Top each piece of fish with 1 ounce of the mustard mixture, and serve.

PER SERVING: 130 calories; 2 g fat (22.5% calories from fat); 8 g protein; 10 g carbohydrate; 1 g dietary fiber; 20 mg cholesterol; 49 mg sodium. Exchanges: 1 lean meat; 1 vegetable; 0 fruit; 0 fat; ½ other carbohydrates.

Grilled Shrimp

Orange and lemon marinated shrimp grilled to perfection

SERVINGS: 4

1 pound jumbo shrimp, *peeled*
2 cloves fresh garlic, *minced*
2 teaspoons olive oil
2 tablespoons hot sauce
¼ cup fresh lemon juice
¼ cup fresh orange juice
¼ cup scallion, *chopped fine*
2 tablespoons fresh dill, *chopped fine*
4 skewers
salt, *to taste*
cracked black pepper, *to taste*

SERVING IDEA:
**Great with fresh
steamed couscous.**

Peel jumbo shrimp, and place 4 ounces of shrimp on each skewer.

Next, place skewered shrimp into an airtight container, and add remaining ingredients.

Let marinate at least 2 hours.

Place shrimp on grill over medium coals, and cook 3 minutes each side. Shrimp may take longer depending on size.

PER SERVING: 156 calories; 4 g fat (25.3% calories from fat); 23 g protein; 5 g carbohydrate; trace dietary fiber; 173 mg cholesterol; 356 mg sodium. Exchanges: 3 lean meat; 0 vegetable; 0 fruit; ½ fat.

Saffron Scallops

Scallops sautéed with tomatoes, garlic and saffron

SERVINGS: 6

1 tablespoon olive oil
1 pound scallops, *shelled and deveined*
¼ cup onion, *finely chopped*
2 cloves garlic, *chopped*
3 tablespoons sherry wine
2 cups tomatoes, *chopped*
½ teaspoon paprika
½ teaspoon salt
¼ teaspoon crushed red pepper
6 saffron threads
1 cup dry white wine

SERVING IDEAS:
Garnish with parsley, and serve with brown rice.

Over high heat in large skillet, heat oil until hot. Add scallops; cook, stirring constantly, for 5 minutes. Remove scallops from skillet, and reduce heat to medium-high.

Add onion and garlic; cook, stir occasionally, until onion is tender, about 1 minute. Add sherry; cook just until sherry has been absorbed, about 2 minutes.

Add tomatoes, paprika, salt, red pepper and saffron threads; cook, stirring frequently, until tomatoes are softened, about 3 minutes.

Stir in white wine; simmer uncovered for 5 minutes. Return scallops to skillet, and cook just until heated through, about 3 minutes.

Serve.

NOTE: Chicken can be used instead of scallops.

PER SERVING: 137 calories; 3 g fat (25.3% calories from fat); 14 g protein; 7 g carbohydrate; 1 g dietary fiber; 25 mg cholesterol; 310 mg sodium. Exchanges: 0 grain (starch); 2 lean meat; ½ vegetable; ½ fat.

Salmon Blush

Salmon with capers and a blush-wine cream sauce

SERVINGS: 6

1 pound salmon fillets
2 teaspoons olive oil
1 teaspoon garlic, *chopped*
2 tablespoons capers
¼ cup white wine
¼ cup half-and-half
1 tablespoon fresh parsley
salt and pepper, *to taste*

In a large sauté pan over medium-high heat, heat olive oil.

Once olive oil is heated, add salmon. Sauté for 8 minutes, turning salmon over every 2 minutes.

Next, add garlic, capers, wine and half-and-half. Bring to a low simmer, and let simmer for 4 minutes. Add salt, pepper and parsley.

Serve.

SERVING IDEAS: Garnish with chopped scallions, and serve with a side of whole-wheat pasta.

PER SERVING: 122 calories; 5 g fat (42.4% calories from fat); 15 g protein; 1 g carbohydrate; trace dietary fiber; 43 mg cholesterol; 82 mg sodium. Exchanges: 2 lean meat; 0 vegetable; 0 nonfat milk; ⅓ fat; 0 other carbohydrates.

Scallops au Gratin

Scallops tossed in Havarti-dill cream sauce

SERVINGS: 4

1 pound scallops
1 tablespoon olive oil
1 teaspoon salt
1 teaspoon pepper
1 teaspoon garlic, *minced*
¼ cup burgundy
½ cup skim milk
½ cup Havarti cheese, *shredded*
2 tablespoons fresh dill

SERVING IDEAS:
Garnish with
fresh dill.

In a large sauté pan over high heat, heat olive oil.

In a separate bowl combine salt, pepper and garlic with scallops, and sauté until browned on both sides. Remove scallops from pan.

Return pan to burner, and deglaze with burgundy. Let burgundy reduce by half.

Next, add skim milk, cheese and dill. Bring to a low simmer, stirring pan with plastic spatula to keep the sauce from scorching.

Return scallops to pan, and simmer on low for 2 minutes.

Serve.

PER SERVING: 142 calories; 6 g fat (42.8% calories from fat); 16 g protein; 3 g carbohydrate; trace dietary fiber; 36 mg cholesterol; 555 mg sodium. Exchanges: 0 grain (starch); 2 lean meat; 0 vegetable; 0 nonfat milk; 1 fat.

Shrimp Scampi

Shrimp in garlic-lemon butter

SERVINGS: 6

> 1 pound shrimp, *peeled and deveined*
> 1 tablespoon olive oil
> 1 tablespoon butter
> 1 tablespoon fresh garlic, *chopped*
> 1 tablespoon fresh lemon juice
> 1 teaspoon parsley, *chopped*

SERVING IDEA:
Garnish with fresh Parmesan cheese.

In a large sauté pan, heat butter and olive oil over medium-high heat. Once butter and olive oil are heated, add shrimp.

Sauté shrimp over medium-high heat for 5 minutes. Add garlic, and sauté for 2 minutes.

Finally, add lemon juice and parsley.

Serve.

NOTE: Chicken can be substituted.

PER SERVING: 120 calories; 5 g fat (42.3% calories from fat); 15 g protein; 1 g carbohydrate; trace dietary fiber; 120 mg cholesterol; 132 mg sodium. Exchanges: 2 lean meat; 0 vegetable; 0 fruit; 1 fat.

Summer Scallops Veggie Supreme

Scallops sautéed with fresh veggies

SERVINGS: 6

1 pound bay scallops
1 teaspoon olive oil
1 teaspoon salt
½ teaspoon cracked black pepper
1 medium red onion, *sliced ½ inch thick*
1 medium tomato, *cut into 2-inch pieces*
½ cup black olives, *cut in half*
1 medium zucchini, *cut into 2-inch pieces*
½ teaspoon celery seed
¼ cup fresh lemon juice

SERVING IDEAS:
Top with shredded smoked Gouda cheese and chopped scallions.

In large sauté pan, heat olive oil on medium-high heat.

Next, add scallops and salt and pepper; sauté for 3 minutes. Scallops will begin to brown.

Add onion, tomato, black olives and zucchini. Sauté until onions become clear.

Once onions are tender, add celery seed and lemon juice, and sauté for 3 minutes. Serve.

NOTES: Depending on the size of the scallops, cooking time will vary. Shrimp can also be added.

PER SERVING: 109 calories; 3 g fat (22.0% calories from fat); 14 g protein; 8 g carbohydrate; 2 g dietary fiber; 25 mg cholesterol; 461 mg sodium. Exchanges: 0 grain (starch); 1½ lean meat; ½ vegetable; 0 fruit; ½ fat.

White Albacore Tuna Spread

White albacore tuna with dill and a hint of hot sauce

SERVINGS: 3

> 7 ounces albacore, *canned*
> 2 tablespoons fresh dill weed, *chopped*
> 1 teaspoon hot sauce
> 1 teaspoon garlic, *minced*
> 1 tablespoon fresh lemon juice
> ¼ cup light mayonnaise
> ¼ cup light sour cream
> salt and pepper, *to taste*

SERVING IDEAS:
Garnish with fresh dill and lemon wedges.

Place tuna, dill, hot sauce, garlic and lemon juice in 3-cup food processor.

Puree for 20 seconds. Using a plastic spatula, wipe down the sides of the bowl.

Next, add sour cream, mayonnaise, salt and pepper. Puree for another 30 seconds.

Serve.

NOTES: This spread should be stored in an airtight container. Freshness will keep for 2 days.

PER SERVING: 147 calories; 6 g fat (36.5% calories from fat); 18 g protein; 5 g carbohydrate; trace dietary fiber; 36 mg cholesterol; 405 mg sodium. Exchanges 2½ lean meat; 0 vegetable, 0 fruit; 1 fat; 0 other carbohydrates.

PASTA

No man is lonely eating spaghetti;
it requires so much attention.

—Christopher Morley

Angel Hair with Tomatoes, Basil and Garlic

Intense basil and garlic tossed with angel hair pasta

SERVINGS: 10

1 pound whole-wheat pasta (angel hair), *cooked*
1 tablespoon olive oil
3 cloves garlic, *minced*
5 cups tomatoes, *diced*
1 bunch fresh basil, *chopped*
¾ cup low-sodium chicken broth
5 tablespoons Parmesan cheese
salt and freshly ground pepper, *to taste*

SERVING IDEAS:
Serve with grilled fish or chicken.

Prepare pasta according to package directions; drain.

Heat oil in a large skillet over medium-high heat. Add garlic, and cook for 1 minute.

Add tomatoes, basil, salt and pepper. Cook for 3 minutes.

Add hot pasta to skillet; toss well. Add chicken broth, and stir.

Toss with Parmesan cheese, and serve immediately.

PER SERVING: 214 calories; 3 g fat (13.6% calories from fat); 8 g protein; 39 g carbohydrate; 2 g dietary fiber; 2 mg cholesterol; 61 mg sodium. Exchanges: 2½ grain (starch); 0 lean meat; 1 vegetable; ½ fat.

Chef Dave's
Asiago Baked Manicotti

*Cheese, garlic, and spices blended and stuffed into pasta
and baked to perfection*

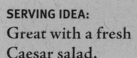

SERVINGS: 8

8 ounces whole-wheat manicotti, *uncooked*
1 15-ounce container part-skim ricotta cheese,
   whipped until smooth
½ cup Asiago cheese, *grated*
2 cloves garlic
¼ cup sliced scallions, *chopped fine*
2 teaspoons Italian seasoning
1 26-ounce jar spaghetti sauce
grated Parmesan cheese, *for topping*

1 egg, *beaten*
2 teaspoons parsley flakes
¼ teaspoon pepper
½ teaspoon salt

SERVING IDEA:
Great with a fresh
Caesar salad.

Prepare pasta according to package directions; drain.

In medium bowl, blend ricotta, Asiago, garlic, egg, scallions and Italian seasoning.

Stir in parsley, salt and pepper.

Stuff pasta with cheese mixture.

Arrange in a 13 × 9 inch baking dish.

Pour spaghetti sauce evenly over pasta.

Sprinkle with Parmesan cheese. Cover.

Bake in a 350°F oven until hot, about 35 minutes.

NOTE: Manicotti is a dish of large pasta tubes stuffed with chopped meat or mild cheese and baked in tomato sauce

PER SERVING: 317 calories; 12 g fat (33.0% calories from fat); 14 g protein; 39 g carbohydrate;
4 g dietary fiber; 49 mg cholesterol; 755 mg sodium. Exchanges: 1½ grain (starch);
1 lean meat; 3 vegetable; 1½ fat.

Mushroom, Pasta, and Chicken Scampi

Garlic chicken with mushrooms and spinach

SERVINGS: 12

8 ounces whole-wheat linguine
1 tablespoon olive oil
½ pound fresh white mushrooms, *sliced*
1 tablespoon garlic, *chopped*
1 pound chicken, *julienned*
10 ounces fresh spinach, *trimmed and torn into pieces*
½ cup chicken stock
¼ cup grated Parmesan cheese
¼ teaspoon crushed red pepper, *if desired*
salt and pepper, *to taste*

> **SERVING IDEA:**
> Garnish with fresh chopped spinach.

Cook linguine according to package directions; drain pasta; set aside.

Meanwhile, heat olive oil in a large skillet. Add mushrooms and garlic; cook and stir until tender and liquid is almost evaporated, about 5 minutes.

Add chicken, and cover and cook until chicken is almost cooked through, about 5 minutes.

Stir in spinach and ½ cup chicken stock; cover and cook until spinach is wilted, about 1 minute.

Place pasta in a bowl; stir in mushroom and chicken mixture, red pepper (optional), and Parmesan cheese; toss to combine. Season with salt, if desired.

NOTE: Shrimp or scallops can be used.

PER SERVING: 158 calories; 6 g fat (36.3% calories from fat); 9 g protein; 16 g carbohydrate; 1 g dietary fiber; 26 mg cholesterol; 160 mg sodium. Exchanges: 1 grain (starch); 1 lean meat; ½ vegetable; ½ fat.

Rigatoni à la Vodka

Rigatoni pasta with a marinara cream sauce with a hint of vodka

SERVINGS: 8

1 pound whole-wheat rigatoni, *cooked and drained*
2 teaspoons olive oil
2 tablespoons garlic, *chopped*
¼ cup chicken stock
½ bunch basil, *chopped*
3 cups marinara sauce
¼ cup half-and-half
¼ cup vodka

SERVING IDEA:
Add Parmesan cheese for the perfect added touch.

In a large sauté pan, heat olive oil; once olive oil is heated, add garlic and sauté for 1 minute.

Next, add chicken stock, and let simmer for 1 minute. Add pasta and marinara sauce and bring to a simmer.

Once pasta and sauce are simmering, add half-and-half, basil and vodka, and let simmer lightly for 3 minutes.

Remove from heat, and serve.

NOTE: Chicken, beef, or pork can be added.

PER SERVING: 391 calories; 5 g fat (11.8% calories from fat); 10 g protein; 51 g carbohydrate; 6 g dietary fiber; 3 mg cholesterol; 461 mg sodium. Exchanges. 3½ grain (starch); 0 vegetable; 0 nonfat milk; 1 fat.

Rotini Sauté

Rotini pasta sautéed with veggies and fresh basil

SERVINGS: 15

1 pound whole-wheat rotini, *cooked and drained*
1 cup plum tomatoes, *chopped*
1 cup broccoli, *cut up*
1 cup baby carrots
1 bunch scallions, *chopped*
¼ cup olive oil
2 tablespoons garlic, *chopped*
1 teaspoon thyme
1 bunch basil, *chopped*
½ cup white wine
salt and pepper, *to taste*

SERVING IDEAS:
Great topped with grilled chicken or shrimp.

In a large sauté pan over high heat, add olive oil. Once olive oil is hot, add garlic and thyme, and sauté for 20 seconds.

Next, add all vegetables, and sauté for 5 minutes. Add cooked rotini, basil, salt, and pepper. Sauté for 5 minutes.

Serve.

PER SERVING: 162 calories; 4 g fat (24.2% calories from fat); 4 g protein; 25 g carbohydrate; 1 g dietary fiber; 0 mg cholesterol; 11 mg sodium. Exchanges: 1½ grain (starch); ½ vegetable; ½ fat.

Shrimp and Scallop Linguine Primavera

Shrimp and scallops tossed with veggies in a garlic, basil butter sauce

SERVINGS: 10

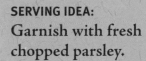

½ pound shrimp, *peeled and deveined*
½ pound sea scallops
¼ cup flour
¼ cup mushrooms, *sliced*
¼ cup scallions, *chopped*
¼ cup plum tomatoes, *diced*
2 tablespoons garlic, *chopped*
1 tablespoon olive oil
¼ stick butter
¼ bunch fresh basil, *chopped*
salt and pepper, *to taste*
1 lemon, *juiced*
½ cup white wine
½ pound whole-wheat linguine, *cooked and drained*

SERVING IDEA:
Garnish with fresh chopped parsley.

To a large sauté pan over medium heat, add butter and olive oil.

Dust scallops with flour.

Once butter and olive oil are hot, add shrimp and dusted scallops, and sauté for 5 minutes.

Next, add mushrooms, scallions, tomatoes, garlic and lemon juice. Sauté for 2 minutes.

Add white wine, salt, pepper and fresh basil. Bring to a simmer for 2 minutes.

Add pasta, and toss with seafood and vegetables. Serve.

PER SERVING: 186 calories; 5 g fat (23.6% calories from fat); 12 g protein; 22 g carbohydrate; 1 g dietary fiber; 48 mg cholesterol; 97 mg sodium. Exchanges: 1½ grain (starch); 1 lean meat; 0 vegetable; 0 fruit; ½ fat.

Spaghetti Veggies

Whole-wheat spaghetti sautéed with mixed vegetables

SERVINGS: 10

½ pound whole-wheat spaghetti, *cooked*
1 tablespoon olive oil
2 cloves garlic, *minced*
2 medium yellow squash, *chopped*
2 medium zucchini, *chopped*
1 small onion, *chopped*
2 cups pea pods
¼ cup lemon juice
½ bunch fresh basil, *chopped*
salt and pepper, *to taste*

SERVING IDEAS:
Great with chicken, fish, or pork side dishes.

Cook pasta according to package; drain, and set aside.

To a large sauté pan over medium-high heat, add olive oil. Once olive oil is heated, add garlic and onion, and sauté for 1 minute.

Next, add yellow squash, zucchini, and pea pods, and sauté for 5 minutes.

Add lemon juice, salt, pepper and basil, and sauté for an additional 2 minutes.

Toss in cooked whole-wheat spaghetti, and sauté for an additional 2 minutes.

Serve.

PER SERVING: 113 calories; 2 g fat (13.4% calories from fat); 5 g protein; 22 g carbohydrate; 3 g dietary fiber; 0 mg cholesterol; 5 mg sodium. Exchanges: 1 grain (starch); 1 vegetable; 0 fruit; ½ fat.

Tuscan Lobster Farfalle

Sautéed lobster with bow-tie pasta and veggies

SERVINGS: 8

1 pound lobster
2 tablespoons butter
1 tablespoon capers
1 tablespoon fresh garlic, *chopped*
½ large red bell pepper, *julienned*
½ cup green olives, *cut in half*
½ cup fresh tomatoes, *diced*
½ bunch fresh oregano, *chopped*
¼ cup fresh lemon juice
½ pound whole-wheat bow-tie pasta, *cooked and drained*
salt and pepper, *to taste*

1 tablespoon olive oil
1 bunch scallions, *chopped*
½ cup black olives, *cut in half*
½ bunch fresh basil, *chopped*

SERVING IDEAS:
Garnish with fresh parsley and Parmesan cheese.

First, cook pasta according to package; drain, and set aside.

To a large sauté pan over medium-high heat, add butter and olive oil. Once olive oil and butter are hot, add garlic, capers and scallions, and sauté for 3 minutes.

Next, add lobster, and sauté for 5 minutes.

Then, add green and red bell pepper, green and black olives, and tomatoes, and sauté for 5 minutes.

Finally, add fresh herbs, lemon juice and pasta, and sauté for 3 minutes. Add salt and pepper to taste. Serve.

NOTE: Scallops and/or chicken can be used in this dish.

PER SERVING: 70 calories; 3 g fat (42.5% calories from fat); 7 g protein; 3 g carbohydrate; 1 g dietary fiber; 38 mg cholesterol; 225 mg sodium. Exchanges: 0 grain (starch); 1 lean meat; 0 vegetable; 0 fruit; ½ fat; 0 other carbohydrates.

PORK

Nothing helps scenery
like ham and eggs.

—**Mark Twain**

CookWise

Oven-Roasted Blackened Pork Tenderloin

Pork with blackening seasoning, topped with a white wine cream sauce.

SERVINGS: 10

2 pounds pork tenderloin, *cut 1 inch thick*
2 tablespoons olive oil
1 teaspoon garlic powder
1 teaspoon onion powder
2 teaspoons paprika
1½ teaspoons salt
1 teaspoon cracked black pepper
¼ teaspoon cumin
1 teaspoon dried thyme
¼ cup dry white wine

SERVING IDEAS: Garnish with paprika and chopped parsley. Beef and chicken can be substituted.

Preheat oven to 350°F.

In a small bowl, combine olive oil, garlic powder, onion powder, paprika, salt, cumin and dried thyme. Mix well, and with a brush apply spice mixture over tenderloin.

Next, pour white wine into the roasting pan. (The wine will keep the juices fr ing to the bottom of the pan and makes a great juice for the pork.)

Place seasoned pork loin into a shallow baking dish on a roasting rack (a baki rack will work).

Place into oven at 350°F. Roast uncovered for 35 minutes or until internal ten reaches 160°F.

Remove from oven, and let rest for 5 minutes. Serve.

NOTE: To make dish spicier, add ½ teaspoon cayenne pepper to seasoning mix.

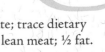

PER SERVING: 141 calories; 6 g fat (39.6% calories from fat); 19 g protein; 1 g carbohydrate; trace dietary fiber; 59 mg cholesterol; 366 mg sodium. Exchanges: 0 grain (starch); 2½ lean meat; ½ fat.

Pork Basil Roll with Herbed Cream Sauce

Pork stuffed with ricotta cheese and fresh basil

SERVINGS: 6

1 pound boneless pork loin, *cut into 6-inch pieces and pounded thin*
½ cup part-skim ricotta cheese
1 bunch basil, *stems removed*
1 tablespoon granulated garlic   1 teaspoon salt
1 teaspoon cracked black pepper   1 tablespoon olive oil

Herb Cream Sauce

3 tablespoons white wine
½ teaspoon garlic, *chopped*   ½ teaspoon thyme, *chopped*
½ teaspoon basil, *chopped*   ½ cup Parmesan cheese
½ cup skim milk   salt and pepper, *to taste*

SERVING IDEA:
Garnish with fresh basil and paprika.

Season pounded pork with garlic, salt and pepper on both sides.

Next, divide ricotta cheese into 6 equal portions. Spread ricotta cheese over 1 side of each portion of pork.

Next, lay whole basil leaves over top of ricotta cheese. Starting at one end, roll pork tightly, cheese side up.

To a large sauté pan over medium heat, add olive oil. Once olive oil is hot, add the stuffed pork rolls, and sauté. Turn pork rolls to brown evenly. Pork rolls will take 5 to 8 minutes to cook. Remove pork rolls from sauté pan.

Pour white wine into sauté pan to deglaze the pan, and add garlic. Add skim milk, and let simmer for 1 minute. Add thyme, basil and cheese. Let simmer for 1 minute; add salt and pepper. Place pork rolls back into pan to reheat in sauce. Serve.

NOTE: Use a toothpick to hold the pork roll together while cooking.

PER SERVING: 99 calories; 6 g fat (56.1% calories from fat); 6 g protein; 4 g carbohydrate; 1 g dietary fiber; 12 mg cholesterol; 517 mg sodium. Exchanges: 0 grain (starch); ½ lean meat; 0 vegetable; 0 nonfat milk; ½ fat.

Pork Chardonnay

Pork sautéed in a white wine sauce

SERVINGS: 8

8 4-ounce pork loin chops, *pounded ¼ inch thick*
1 teaspoon salt and pepper
¼ cup flour
2 teaspoons dried thyme
2 teaspoons paprika
3 tablespoons olive oil
½ cup white wine
2 tomatoes, *peeled and chopped*
½ cup fresh mushrooms, *sliced*
½ cup scallions, *chopped*
1 clove fresh garlic, *chopped*
½ cup chicken stock

SERVING IDEA:
Serve over a bed of
spaghetti vegetables.

First, salt and pepper pork loin chops. Next, add thyme and paprika to flour, and lightly coat pork chops with seasoned flour.

Place olive oil in large sauté pan on medium-high heat. Once olive oil is heated, add coated pork chops, and sauté until pork is golden brown.

When pork chops are browned on both sides, add white wine to deglaze the pan.

Next, add tomatoes, mushrooms, scallions, garlic and chicken stock to pan.

Let pork dish simmer for 10 minutes or until pork is cooked. The stock will become thickened while cooking.

Serve.

PER SERVING: 180 calories; 9 g fat (49.3% calories from fat); 15 g protein; 6 g carbohydrate; 1 g dietary fiber; 36 mg cholesterol; 346 mg sodium. Exchanges: 0 grain (starch); 2 lean meat; ½ vegetable; 1 fat.

Pork Stir-Fry

Pork sautéed with veggies and sesame oil.

SERVINGS: 6

1 pound pork loin, *cut into thin strips*
¼ cup broccoli florets
¼ cup carrot, *julienned*
¼ cup onion, *julienned*
¼ cup bamboo shoots, *sliced*
¼ cup baby corn
¼ cup pea pods
¼ cup soy sauce
1 tablespoon sesame oil
1 teaspoon ground ginger
1 teaspoon garlic powder
black pepper, *to taste*

SERVING IDEAS:
Serve over brown rice, and top with scallions.

Place pork, soy sauce, sesame oil, ginger, garlic and pepper into a self-sealing plastic bag. Let marinate for 30 minutes.

Next, heat a large sauté pan over high heat. Once sauté pan is hot, add pork. Sauté pork for 4 minutes, turning every minute.

Next, add vegetables, and sauté for 5 minutes or until pork is done.

Serve.

NOTE: This stir-fry can be made with chicken or beef also.

PER SERVING: 104 calories; 5 g fat (43.4% calories from fat); 11 g protein; 4 g carbohydrate; 1 g dietary fiber; 24 mg cholesterol; 709 mg sodium. Exchanges: 0 grain (starch); 1½ lean meat; ½ vegetable; ½ fat.

Pork Tenderloin
with Cointreau and Ginger

Ginger and garlic with a hint of lime and red pepper

SERVINGS: 6

1½ pounds pork tenderloin
2 tablespoons olive oil
¼ cup Cointreau or other orange liqueur
2 tablespoons ginger, *minced*
2 tablespoons soy sauce
1 teaspoon garlic, *minced*
2 tablespoons green onions, *minced*
1 tablespoon lime juice
½ teaspoon red pepper flakes (optional)
½ cup beef broth

SERVING IDEA:
Great with
wild rice.

Place tenderloin in a plastic bag; put all ingredients except beef broth in bag with pork. Rub to coat pork well. Chill for several hours. Remove pork from bag, and reserve marinade.

Preheat sauté pan over medium heat. Sauté pork over medium heat for about 20 minutes or until done. Baste frequently with marinade.

Reserve all juices. Combine beef broth with a ½ cup of reserved marinade. Heat to a boil. Simmer 5 minutes. Add pork juices. Simmer for a few minutes.

Slice tenderloin. Arrange on plates, pour warm sauce over slices. Garnish with cilantro and orange slices, if desired.

PER SERVING: 188 calories; 8 g fat (41.4% calories from fat); 25 g protein; 2 g carbohydrate; trace dietary fiber; 74 mg cholesterol; 507 mg sodium. Exchanges: 0 grain (starch); 3½ lean meat; 0 vegetable; 0 fruit; 1 fat.

Sausage and Potato Hot Pot

A quick and easy one-pot meal

SERVINGS: 10

2 teaspoons vegetable oil
2 small onions, *sliced thin*
1 pound Italian sausage, *cut into 2-inch pieces*
1 pound potatoes, *thinly sliced*
2 tablespoons mustard
1 cup chicken stock
salt and pepper, *to taste*

SERVING IDEAS:
Garnish with fresh grated low-fat cheddar cheese and diced scallions.

Heat oil in large frying pan with a lid.

Add onions and sausages until they start to brown.

Next, add potato slices, and stir into onion and sausage mixture.

Continue cooking until potatoes begin to brown.

Add chicken stock and mustard; cover with lid, and cook for 10 minutes or until potatoes are tender.

Remove lid, and add cheese.

Salt and pepper to taste.

Serve.

NOTE: I use mild sausage, but use hot if you like it spicy.

PER SERVING: 214 calories; 15 g fat (65.1% calories from fat); 8 g protein; 11 g carbohydrate; 1 g dietary fiber; 35 mg cholesterol; 588 mg sodium. Exchanges: ½ grain (starch); 1 lean meat; ½ vegetable; 2½ fat; 0 other carbohydrates.

Sausage Couscous

Sausage and couscous in a tasty one-pot meal

SERVINGS: 8

1 pound Italian sausage, *ground*
1 large tomato, *chopped*
½ cup scallions
2 cloves garlic, *minced*
½ cup green bell pepper, *chopped*
1 cup couscous
2½ cups chicken stock
1 bunch fresh basil
salt and pepper, *to taste*

SERVING IDEAS:
Serve with roasted red pepper and mushrooms.

In a medium sauce pot over medium heat, add Italian sausage, scallions, tomatoes, garlic and green bell peppers.

Sauté for 5 minutes. Drain off any excess grease.

Add couscous, chicken stock and fresh basil. Bring mixture to a simmer, and cook according to the directions on the couscous package. Salt and pepper.

Serve immediately, or chill and eat cold.

NOTE: The amount of chicken stock may need to be adjusted according to couscous package directions.

PER SERVING: 293 calories; 18 g fat (56.8% calories from fat); 11 g protein; 19 g carbohydrate; 2 g dietary fiber; 43 mg cholesterol; 1,091 mg sodium. Exchanges: 1 grain (starch); 1 lean meat; ½ vegetable; 3 fat.

POULTRY

Poultry is like meat, except when you cook it rare. Then it's like bird-flavored Jell-O.

—P. J. O'Rourke

Blue Cheese and Cheddar Chicken

*Chicken stuffed with blue cheese and
smothered in cheddar cheese sauce*

SERVINGS: 6

6 large boneless, skinless chicken breasts, *pounded thin*
4 ounces blue cheese, *crumbled*
1 tablespoon granulated garlic
1 teaspoon salt   1 tablespoon black pepper

SERVING IDEAS:
Great with fresh
steamed carrots
and broccoli.

Cheesy Cream Sauce

1 tablespoon butter   1 teaspoon garlic, *chopped*
1 tablespoon flour   1 cup skim milk
¾ cup low-fat cheddar   ¼ cup white wine
   cheese, *shredded*   salt and pepper, *to taste*

Season pounded chicken breast on both sides with salt, pepper and garlic.

Next, divide blue cheese evenly into six portions, and smear one side of seasoned chicken breasts.

Roll chicken breasts cheese side up, and tuck ends under.

Bake in a preheated oven at 350°F for 35 to 40 minutes.

To prepare sauce, melt butter over medium heat in a medium saucepan. Add garlic, and sauté for 2 minutes.

Next, add flour to butter and garlic, and cook for 2 minutes. Add skim milk, and stir until sauce begins to simmer. Sauce will begin to thicken. Add white wine and cheddar cheese, and cook at a low simmer for 5 minutes. Salt and pepper to taste.

Once chicken is done, pour cream sauce over chicken. Serve.

NOTE: Use a toothpick to hold chicken roll together while cooking.

PER SERVING: 401 calories; 11 g fat (26.9% calories from fat); 64 g protein; 6 g carbohydrate; trace dietary fiber; 160 mg cholesterol; 901 mg sodium. Exchanges: 0 grain (starch); 8½ lean meat; 0 vegetable; 0 nonfat milk; 1 fat.

Chicken Cacciatore Meatballs

All the taste of chicken cacciatore with a new twist

SERVINGS: 6

1 pound ground chicken
½ cup seasoned bread crumbs
¼ cup grated Parmesan cheese
2 tablespoons fresh parsley, *chopped*
¼ cup white wine
1 large egg
3 teaspoons black olives, *chopped*
2 cloves garlic, *minced*
½ teaspoon dried basil
½ teaspoon salt
¼ teaspoon pepper
4 cups tomato sauce (*canned and not seasoned*)

SERVING IDEAS:
Great stuffed between whole-wheat pita with low-fat mozzarella cheese.

In a large bowl, thoroughly combine ground chicken, bread crumbs, Parmesan cheese, egg, parsley, white wine, black olives, garlic, basil, salt and pepper.

Form into 1½-inch meatballs.

To a large pot, add tomato sauce, and bring to a light simmer.

Add meatballs to sauce, and let simmer covered for 25 minutes or until meatballs are thoroughly cooked. *Do not stir* for 10 minutes or meatballs may break apart.

NOTE: Ground turkey can be substituted for chicken.

PER SERVING: 116 calories; 2 g fat (15.8% calories from fat); 20 g protein, 8 g carbohydrate; 1 g dietary fiber; 47 mg cholesterol; 568 mg sodium. Exchanges: ½ grain (starch); 2½ lean meat; 0 vegetable; 0 fruit; 0 fat.

Chicken Valencia

Chicken simmered with fresh garlic, scallions, tomatoes and mushrooms

SERVINGS: 8

8 boneless, skinless chicken breasts, *pounded thin*
1 teaspoon salt
1 teaspoon pepper
¼ cup flour
3 tablespoons olive oil
½ cup white wine
2 tomatoes, *peeled and chopped*
½ cup fresh mushrooms, *sliced*
½ cup scallions, *chopped*
1 clove fresh garlic, *chopped*
½ cup chicken stock

SERVING IDEAS:
Serve over whole-wheat pasta and fresh steamed green beans.

First, salt and pepper chicken breasts.

Next, lightly coat chicken breasts with flour.

Then, place olive oil in a large sauté pan on medium-high heat. Once olive oil is heated, add coated chicken breast, and sauté until chicken is golden brown.

When chicken is browned on both sides, add white wine to deglaze the pan.

Then, add tomatoes, mushrooms, scallions, garlic, and chicken stock to pan.

Let chicken dish simmer for 10 minutes or until chicken is cooked. The stock will become thickened while cooking.

NOTE: Chicken stock can be used in place of white wine.

PER SERVING: 340 calories; 8 g fat (23.2% calories from fat); 55 g protein; 5 g carbohydrate; 1 g dietary fiber; 137 mg cholesterol; 470 mg sodium. Exchanges: 0 grain (starch); 7½ lean meat; ½ vegetable; 1 fat.

Greek Meatballs

Ground turkey with garlic, mint and oregano

SERVINGS: 6

SERVING IDEA:
**Great with
Greek Bean Salad.**

1 pound ground turkey, *ground*
1 large onion, *minced*
1 large egg
¼ cup dried parsley
2 tablespoons dried oregano
3 tablespoons dried mint flakes
1 teaspoon garlic powder
½ cup seasoned bread crumbs
1 teaspoon salt
1 cup water

First, spray a pan with nonstick cooking spray, and sauté onions until clear and golden.

Next, place all ingredients into a large mixing bowl, including the onions. Mix ingredients well.

Next, shape meat mixture into meatballs, and slightly flatten them.

Bake at 375°F for 25 minutes, turning once. (Smaller meatballs may take less time, and larger meatballs will take longer.)

As soon as meatballs are done, lightly salt them.

NOTE: These meatballs are traditionally made with lamb, but to cut down on the fat, use turkey.

PER SERVING: 151 calories; 2 g fat (11.3% calories from fat); 22 g protein; 11 g carbohydrate; 2 g dietary fiber; 82 mg cholesterol; 678 mg sodium. Exchanges: ½ grain (starch); 2½ lean meat; ½ vegetable; 0 fat.

Orange-Ginger Chicken

Chicken marinated and sautéed with ginger and orange zest

SERVINGS: 4

1 pound boneless, skinless chicken breast, *pounded thin*
1 tablespoon orange zest
¼ cup fresh orange juice
2 teaspoons grated ginger root
1 tablespoon sesame oil
1 bunch scallions, *chopped*
1 teaspoon garlic, *chopped*
1 tablespoon olive oil
salt and pepper, *to taste*

SERVING IDEA:
Garnish with fresh chopped parsley.

Place all ingredients into a self-sealing plastic bag, and marinate for 1 to 8 hours.

Remove chicken from marinade.

To a large sauté pan over medium heat, add olive oil.

Once olive oil is heated, add chicken, and sauté 4 to 5 minutes.

Serve.

NOTES: This marinade is great for seafood and fish. Tastes great grilled!

PER SERVING: 156 calories; 4 g fat (22.3% calories from fat); 26 g protein; 3 g carbohydrate; trace dietary fiber; 66 mg cholesterol; 75 mg sodium. Exchanges: 3½ lean meat; 0 vegetable; 0 fruit; ½ fat.

Poblano Chicken

Chicken sautéed with poblano peppers

SERVINGS SIZE: 4

> 1 pound boneless, skinless chicken breast, *pounded thin*
> ½ teaspoon chili powder
> ½ teaspoon cumin
> 1 small poblano pepper, *diced small*
> 1 tablespoon olive oil
> 1 teaspoon garlic, *chopped*
> ¼ cup white wine
> 2 tablespoons lemon juice
> 2 tablespoons fresh cilantro, *chopped*
> salt and pepper, *to taste*

SERVING IDEA:
Garnish with fresh-grated Monterey Jack cheese.

In a large sauté pan over medium-high heat, add olive oil.

Season chicken breast with chili powder, cumin, salt and pepper.

Once olive oil is hot, place pounded chicken breast into pan, and sauté for 2 minutes on each side.

Next, add chopped poblano pepper and garlic, and sauté for 2 minutes; add white wine to deglaze pan.

Finally, add lemon juice and cilantro.

Serve.

NOTE: Shrimp and scallops can be substituted for chicken.

PER SERVING: 176 calories; 5 g fat (27.3% calories from fat); 27 g protein; 3 g carbohydrate; trace dietary fiber; 66 mg cholesterol; 80 mg sodium. Exchanges: 0 grain (starch); 3½ lean meat; ½ vegetable; 0 fruit; ½ fat.

Ricotta Chicken

Chicken stuffed with pine nuts and sun-dried tomatoes,
and finished with white wine

SERVINGS: 4

1 pound boneless, skinless chicken breast,
    pounded ¼ inch thick
½ cup part–skim milk mozzarella cheese
2 tablespoons pine nuts (pignoli)
2 tablespoons fresh basil, *chopped*
1 tablespoon fresh thyme, *chopped*
2 tablespoons sun-dried tomatoes, *chopped*
1 artichoke heart, *chopped*
½ cup white wine
salt and pepper, *to taste*

SERVING IDEAS:
Garnish with diced sun-dried tomatoes and fresh basil.

Preheat oven to 350°F.

Next, in a large bowl combine mozzarella cheese, pine nuts, basil, thyme, sun-dried tomatoes and artichoke hearts. Mix well.

Lay pounded chicken breasts flat, and divide cheese filling evenly.

Spread cheese mixture over top of chicken breasts, and roll each chicken breast tightly, cheese side up.

Place chicken breasts seam side down into a baking pan.

Next, pour white wine into baking dish with chicken, and add salt and pepper.

Bake at 350°F for 20 minutes or until done and juices run clear. Serve.

NOTE: Chicken stock can be used instead of white wine.

PER SERVING: 224 calories; 6 g fat (27.1% calories from fat); 32 g protein; 5 g carbohydrate; 2 g dietary fiber; 73 mg cholesterol; 203 mg sodium. Exchanges: 0 grain (starch); 4½ lean meat; ½ vegetable; ½ fat.

Sage-Dijon Turkey Meatballs

Ground turkey with sage in a Dijon mustard sauce

SERVINGS: 4

1 pound ground turkey
1 teaspoon dried sage
½ teaspoon dried basil
½ teaspoon dried oregano
2 tablespoons olive oil
1 clove garlic, *minced*
¼ cup Asiago cheese
1 egg
¼ cup white wine
½ cup skim milk
2 tablespoons Dijon mustard
salt and pepper, *to taste*

SERVING IDEAS:
Garnish with chopped sage and fresh ground pepper.

In a large mixing bowl, combine turkey, sage, basil, oregano, garlic, cheese, egg, salt and pepper. Mix well.

Next, divide meat mixture into 8 even pieces, and roll into 8 round balls.

Next, in a large sauté pan over medium-high heat, add olive oil. Once olive oil is hot, add meatballs, and sauté for 10 minutes. Turn frequently to brown all sides of the meatballs.

Drain grease from pan, return to heat, and deglaze with white wine. Add mustard and skim milk, and bring to a simmer. Let simmer for 7 minutes. Serve.

PER SERVING: 93 calories, 6 g fat (63.3% calories from fat); 5 g protein; 3 g carbohydrate; trace dietary fiber; 60 mg cholesterol; 214 mg sodium. Exchanges: 0 grain (starch); ½ lean meat; 0 vegetable; 0 nonfat milk; 1 fat; 0 other carbohydrates.

Turkey Fajitas

Turkey spiced with seasoned peppers and onions

SERVINGS: 8

1 pound boneless, skinless turkey breast,
  cut into thin strips
1 tablespoon olive oil
2 cloves fresh garlic, *peeled and minced*
1 medium onion, *cut into thin strips*
1 large green bell pepper, *cut into thin strips*
1 tablespoon chili powder
1 teaspoon cumin powder
½ teaspoon salt
½ teaspoon white pepper

SERVING IDEAS:
Top with sharp low-fat cheddar cheese and a dollop of light sour cream.

Add olive oil to a preheated pan. Once oil is heated, add turkey, and sauté for 5 minutes.

Next, add garlic, onion, green bell pepper and remaining seasonings.

Mix well, and sauté until turkey is done, approximately 8 minutes.

Serve.

NOTES: To add more spice, top with hot sauce. Turkey can be replaced with beef or pork.

PER SERVING: 93 calories; 2 g fat (23.0% calories from fat); 14 g protein; 3 g carbohydrate; 1 g dietary fiber; 35 mg cholesterol; 172 mg sodium. Exchanges: 0 grain (starch); 1½ lean meat; ½ vegetable; ½ fat.

Turkey Tacos

Ground turkey seasoned with traditional Mexican spices

SERVINGS: 4

> 1 pound ground turkey
> 1 tablespoon olive oil
> ¼ cup onion, *peeled and chopped*
> 2 cloves garlic, *minced*
> 1 teaspoon cumin
> 1 teaspoon chili powder
> ¼ cup tomato sauce
> salt and pepper, *to taste*

SERVING IDEAS:
Garnish with low-fat cheddar cheese and light sour cream.

In a large sauté pan over medium heat, add olive oil.

Once olive oil is heated, add ground turkey, onion and garlic, and sauté for 5 minutes.

Drain any fat from the pan, and return to heat.

Add remaining ingredients, and bring to a simmer. Let simmer for 8 minutes.

Serve.

NOTE: Ground beef and ground pork can be substituted for turkey.

PER SERVING: 170 calories; 4 g fat (23.9% calories from fat); 28 g protein; 3 g carbohydrate; 1 g dietary fiber; 70 mg cholesterol; 156 mg sodium. Exchanges: 0 grain (starch); 3½ lean meat; ½ vegetable; ½ fat.

Vermouth Chicken

Sautéed chicken in a vermouth herbed sauce

SERVINGS: 4

1 pound boneless, skinless chicken breast, *pounded thin*
1 tablespoon olive oil   ¼ cup vermouth
1 cup chicken stock   3 teaspoons butter
1 tablespoon fresh basil, *chopped*
1 tablespoon fresh thyme, *chopped*
1 tablespoon fresh marjoram, *chopped*
1 tablespoon fresh parsley, *chopped*
2 tablespoons fresh lemon juice
salt and pepper, *to taste*

SERVING IDEA:
Garnish with fresh chopped herbs.

Season chicken breast with salt and pepper.

Heat olive oil in a large skillet over high heat until hot.

Add chicken, and sauté for 2 to 3 minutes, until browned.

Transfer cooked chicken to a plate. Cover, and keep warm.

Pour off the oil from the pan.

Stir in the vermouth, scrapping up any browned particles from the bottom and sides of the pan. Add chicken stock, and bring to a boil over high heat.

Reduce the heat, and simmer for 4 minutes, until reduced to ¼ cup. Lower heat, and whisk in butter 1 teaspoon at a time. Then add the herbs and lemon juice, and season lightly with salt and pepper.

NOTE: Substitute shrimp or scallops for chicken.

PER SERVING: 212 calories; 8 g fat (37.7% calories from fat); 27 g protein; 2 g carbohydrate; trace dietary fiber; 74 mg cholesterol; 645 mg sodium. Exchanges: 0 grain (starch); 3½ lean meat; 0 vegetable; 0 fruit; 1½ fat.

SALAD DRESSINGS AND SAUCES

Woe to the cook
whose sauce has no sting.
—Geoffrey Chaucer

Corn Dressing

SERVINGS: 6

> 2 cups fresh corn
> ½ cup olive oil
> ¼ cup fresh lemon juice
> ¼ bunch cilantro, *finely chopped*
> 2 cloves garlic, *minced*

Place ingredients in a blender. Blend.

Chill and serve.

PER SERVING: 49 calories; 1 g fat (9.7% calories from fat); 2 g protein; 11.0 g carbohydrate; 1 g dietary fiber; 0 mg cholesterol; 8 mg sodium. Exchanges: ½ grain (starch); 0 lean meat; 0 vegetable; 0 fruit.

Cucumber-Dill Dressing

SERVINGS: 6

3 large cucumbers, *chopped*
1 bunch dill, *diced*
¼ cup fresh lime juice
½ teaspoon cayenne

Add ingredients to a blender. Blend until smooth.

Chill and serve.

NOTE: Add salt to taste.

PER SERVING: 24 calories; trace fat (7.9% calories from fat); 1 g protein; 5 g carbohydrate; 1 g dietary fiber; 0 mg cholesterol; 4 mg sodium. Exchanges: 0 grain (starch); 1 vegetable; 0 fruit; 0 fat.

Death-by-Garlic Sauce

Olive oil, garlic, and lemon juice and then more garlic . . .

SERVINGS: 32

10 cloves garlic, *peeled*
½ cup olive oil
2 tablespoons fresh lemon juice
1 teaspoon salt
½ teaspoon black pepper
½ cup light sour cream

SERVING IDEAS:
Great for dipping
chicken, beef
and seafood.

Place all ingredients except olive oil into a food processor, and process for 2 minutes.

Next, while the food processor is on, add olive oil slowly, to incorporate oil into garlic mixture.

Process for 1 minute. Refrigerate and serve.

NOTES: A blender will not work because the garlic cannot be chopped fine enough in a blender. The longer this sits, the better it becomes.

PER SERVING: 33 calories; 3 g fat (91.8% calories from fat); trace protein; 1 g carbohydrate; trace dietary fiber; trace cholesterol; 68 mg sodium. Exchanges: 0 grain (starch); 0 lean meat; 0 vegetable; 0 fruit; ½ fat; 0 other carbohydrates.

Five-Minute Basil Vinaigrette

A quick fresh basil salad dressing

SERVINGS: 20

⅓ cup chopped fresh basil
2 tablespoons Dijon mustard
1½ teaspoons seasoned salt
¾ teaspoon ground black pepper
½ cup olive oil
⅓ cup white wine vinegar
1 tablespoon fresh lemon juice

SERVING IDEAS:
Great over fresh salad or as a marinade.

In a blender combine basil, mustard, seasoned salt, pepper, vinegar and lemon juice.

Next, turn blender on low, and pour oil in from top slowly.

Blend until all oil has been added.

Refrigerate.

Stir just before using.

PER SERVING: 50 calories; 5 g fat (95.6% calories from fat); trace protein; trace carbohydrate; trace dietary fiber; 0 mg cholesterol; 121 mg sodium. Exchanges: 0 lean meat; 0 vegetable; 0 fruit; 1 fat; 0 other carbohydrates.

Italian Dressing

SERVINGS: 15

½ cup extra-virgin olive oil
¼ cup balsamic vinegar
½ teaspoon dried basil
½ teaspoon dried thyme
½ teaspoon dried oregano
1 clove garlic
salt and pepper, *to taste*

Place all ingredients in a blender. Blend until ingredients are mixed well, about
1 minute.

Chill and serve.

NOTE: Fresh herbs can also be used.

PER SERVING: 65 calories; 7 g fat (97.3% calories from fat); trace protein; trace carbohydrate; trace
dietary fiber; 0 mg cholesterol; trace sodium. Exchanges: 0 grain (starch); 0 vegetable;
0 fruit; 1½ fat.

Lemon Dressing

Fresh lemon juice mixed with garlic and parsley

SERVINGS: 15

½ cup extra-virgin olive oil
¼ cup fresh lemon juice
1 clove garlic, *minced*
¼ bunch parsley, *chopped fine*
salt and pepper, *to taste*

Place all ingredients in a blender. Blend until smooth.

Chill and serve.

PER SERVING: 66 calories; 7 g fat (96.3% calories from fat); trace protein; 1 g carbohydrate; trace
dietary fiber; 0 mg cholesterol; 1 mg sodium. Exchanges: 0 vegetable; 0 fruit; 1½ fat.

81

Mojo Sauce

Cuban sauce with garlic, cumin and oregano

The authentic mojo is made with juice from sour oranges. It still has the orange taste, but it is very acidic and tart. You can come close by mixing equal amounts of freshly squeezed orange juice with lime juice. Some markets may have pre-made bottled mojo, or their produce department may have the slightly bumpy, thick-skinned sour oranges. This recipe makes 1 cup.

⅓ cup olive oil

6 to 8 cloves garlic, *thinly sliced or minced*

⅔ cup sour orange juice or lime juice (or equal portions orange juice and lime juice)

½ teaspoon ground cumin

½ teaspoon dried oregano

salt and freshly ground black pepper, *to taste*

Heat the olive oil in a deep saucepan over medium heat. Add the garlic, and cook until fragrant and lightly toasted.

Add the sour orange juice, cumin, salt and pepper.

Cool before serving.

NOTE: Mojo is best when served within a couple of hours of preparing, but it will keep for several days if well capped in a jar or bottle in the refrigerator.

No-Anchovies Caesar Dressing

All the taste, none of the fish

SERVINGS: 32

1 tablespoon garlic, *chopped*
2 whole eggs, *cracked*
½ cup Parmesan cheese, *grated*
¼ cup red wine vinegar
1½ tablespoons whole-grain mustard
1½ tablespoons Dijon-style mustard
1½ teaspoons Worcestershire sauce
1½ tablespoons salt
½ teaspoon pepper
¾ cup vegetable oil
¾ cup olive oil

SERVING IDEAS:
Great tossed with whole-wheat pasta and four or five chopped veggies that are in season.

Combine the garlic, eggs, cheese, vinegar, mustards, Worcestershire sauce, salt and pepper in the bowl of a food processor, and process until smooth, approximately 1 minute.

With the machine running slowly, begin adding the oils to form an emulsion.

Continue until all the oil is incorporated.

NOTE: If you prefer anchovies, add 1 ounce of anchovies to the food processor. This dressing must be refrigerated.

PER SERVING: 102 calories; 11 g fat (94.1% calories from fat); 1 g protein; trace carbohydrate; trace dietary fiber; 14 mg cholesterol; 348 mg sodium. Exchanges: 0 grain (starch); 0 lean meat; 0 vegetable; 2 fat; 0 other carbohydrates.

Tzatziki

A creamy garlic, cucumber sauce

SERVINGS: 16

16 ounces light sour cream
1 large cucumber, *grated*
2 cloves garlic, *minced*
1 tablespoon vinegar
3 tablespoons oil
salt, *to taste*

SERVING IDEAS:
Great with
Greek Meatballs.

Once cucumber is grated, squeeze out all the moisture.

Place sour cream in a medium bowl.

Add squeezed cucumber, minced garlic, vinegar, oil and salt.

Mix well, and let sit overnight for best flavor.

PER SERVING: 36 calories; 3 g fat (73.5% calories from fat); 1 g protein; 2 g carbohydrate; trace dietary fiber; 2 mg cholesterol; 8 mg sodium. Exchanges: 0 lean meat; 0 vegetable; ½ fat; 0 other carbohydrates.

SALADS

To remember a successful salad
is generally to remember a successful
dinner; at all events, the perfect
dinner necessarily includes
the perfect salad.

—George Ellwanger

Garlic-Lemon Couscous Salad with Shrimp

Couscous tossed with shrimp, lemon and garlic

SERVINGS: 8

2 cups low-sodium chicken broth
1 cup couscous, *uncooked*
1½ cups cherry tomato halves
½ cup fresh parsley, *finely chopped*
8 ounces cooked shrimp
5 tablespoons fresh lemon juice
1 tablespoon olive oil
¼ cup scallions, *chopped*
½ teaspoon garlic powder
½ teaspoon pepper
¼ teaspoon salt

SERVING IDEAS:
Serve chilled.
For more flavor, use grilled shrimp and balsamic vinegar.

Bring chicken broth to a boil in a medium saucepan; stir in couscous.

Remove from heat, and let stand, covered, 5 minutes; fluff with a fork. Uncover, and let cool 10 minutes.

Combine cooked couscous, cherry tomatoes, parsley and shrimp in a large bowl; toss gently.

Combine lemon juice and next 5 ingredients in a small bowl; stir.

Add to couscous mixture; toss to coat.

PER SERVING: 156 calories; 3 g fat (14.6% calories from fat); 13 g protein; 20 g carbohydrate; 2 g dietary fiber; 52 mg cholesterol; 255 mg sodium. Exchanges: 1 grain (starch); 1½ lean meat; ½ vegetable; 0 fruit; ½ fat.

Mandarin Salad

*Romaine and escarole lettuce tossed with
a sweet mandarin-orange dressing*

SERVINGS: 10

Salad dressing

    ½ cup light sour cream
    ½ cup light mayonnaise
    ¼ cup honey
    3 tablespoons apple cider vinegar
    2 8-ounce cans mandarin oranges, *drained*
    1 cup scallions, *chopped*
    1 teaspoon celery salt
    salt and pepper, *to taste*

Lettuce mixture

    4 cups romaine lettuce, *chopped*
    2 cups escarole, *chopped*
    ½ cup walnuts, *chopped*

Place all ingredients except lettuce and walnuts into a large mixing bowl, and mix well.

Add romaine, escarole and walnuts to the mixing bowl.

Toss with salad dressing.

Serve.

PER SERVING: 112 calories; 6 g fat (45.7% calories from fat); 3 g protein; 14 g carbohydrate; 2 g dietary fiber; 5 mg cholesterol; 227 mg sodium. Exchanges: 0 grain (starch); 0 lean meat; ½ vegetable; 0 fruit; 1 fat; ½ other carbohydrates.

Mandarin Orange Salad
with Strawberry Vinaigrette

Mandarin oranges tossed with Romaine, cucumber and strawberries

SERVINGS: 8

4 cups romaine lettuce, *chopped*
1 cup mandarin orange sections, *raw*
¼ cup chopped pecans
½ cup scallions, *chopped*
½ cup grape tomatoes
½ small cucumber, *peeled and chopped*
½ cup fresh strawberries, *pureed*
¼ cup raspberry vinegar
1 tablespoon vegetable oil

SERVING IDEAS:
Great topped
with grilled
chicken or fish.

Place all ingredients into a large mixing bowl, and toss well.

Serve.

NOTE: To ensure that the lettuce does not get soggy, do not toss until ready to serve.

PER SERVING: 53 calories; 3 g fat (50.0% calories from fat); 1 g protein; 6 g carbohydrate; 2 g dietary
fiber; 0 mg cholesterol; 4 mg sodium. Exchanges: 0 grain (starch); 0 lean meat;
½ vegetable; 0 fruit; ½ fat; 0 other carbohydrates.

Seafood Calypso Salad

Shrimp, scallops and crab tossed with calypso dressing

SERVINGS: 12

½ pound shrimp, *cooked*
½ pound scallops, *cooked*
½ pound crab meat
1 teaspoon celery seed
1 teaspoon onion powder
2 cloves garlic, *chopped fine*
1 tablespoon lime juice
½ bunch dill, *chopped*
1 teaspoon hot sauce
¼ cup light mayonnaise
¼ cup light sour cream
¼ cup cocktail sauce
salt and pepper, *to taste*

Place all ingredients in a large mixing bowl. Toss well.

Place in refrigerator, and let chill for 2 hours.

Serve.

NOTE: Fresh cooked fish can also be used.

SERVING IDEAS:
Garnish with lime wedges and chopped dill.

PER SERVING: 76 calories; 2 g fat (22.0% calories from fat); 11 g protein; 3 g carbohydrate; trace dietary fiber; 54 mg cholesterol; 199 mg sodium. Exchanges: 0 grain (starch); 1½ lean meat; 0 vegetable; 0 fruit; 1 fat; 0 other carbohydrates.

Sweet Pea Salad

Sweet peas tossed with bacon, cheese and tomatoes

SERVINGS: 8

3 cups sweet green peas, *cooked*
¼ pound bacon, *cooked crisp and chopped*
1 cup part-skim-milk mozzarella cheese, *shredded*
2 tablespoons olive oil
¼ cup onion, *chopped fine*
2 plum tomatoes, *chopped*
2 cloves garlic, *minced*
½ cup black olives, *halved*
½ cup red bell pepper, *chopped*
½ bunch parsley, *chopped fine*
salt and pepper, *to taste*

SERVING IDEAS:
This dish is great served with grilled chicken and shrimp.

Place all ingredients into a large bowl, and mix well.

Refrigerate for 2 to 3 hours before serving.

PER SERVING: 137 calories; 11 g fat (72.2% calories from fat); 7 g protein; 3 g carbohydrate; 1 g dietary fiber; 16 mg cholesterol; 303 mg sodium. Exchanges: 1 lean meat; ½ vegetable; 0 fruit; 1½ fat.

Watermelon Salad

Watermelon tossed with mint and scallions in raspberry vinaigrette

SERVINGS: 8

2 cups watermelon, *seeded and cubed*
2 teaspoons mint, *chopped*
¼ cup scallions, *chopped*
2 kiwi fruit, *peeled and cubed*
¼ cup fresh lemon juice
¼ cup raspberry vinegar
3 tablespoons Splenda
salt and pepper, *to taste*

SERVING IDEA:
Great with fresh grilled salmon.

Place all ingredients into a large mixing bowl, and toss lightly.

Refrigerate for 4 hours to give the salad a chance to marinate.

Serve.

PER SERVING: 28 calories; trace fat (7.1% calories from fat); 1 g protein; 7 g carbohydrate; 1 g dietary fiber; 0 mg cholesterol; 2 mg sodium. Exchanges: 0 vegetable; ½ fruit; 0 other carbohydrates.

SIDE DISHES

*Vegetables are a must on a diet.
I suggest carrot cake, zucchini bread,
and pumpkin pie.*

—Jim Davis

Creamy Corn Pudding

You have never had corn pudding so creamy and good.

SERVINGS: 12

3 large eggs, *beaten*
1 15.25-ounce can whole kernel corn, *drained*
1 12-ounce can evaporated milk
½ cup dry breadcrumbs, *unseasoned*
1½ tablespoons Splenda
½ teaspoon salt
½ teaspoon black pepper
½ teaspoon paprika
½ teaspoon garlic powder
½ teaspoon onion powder

SERVING IDEAS:
Great with Champagne-Poached Salmon.

Preheat oven to 350°F.

Using nonstick spray, coat a 1½- to 2-quart casserole dish.

In large bowl, combine all ingredients.

Pour into casserole; place casserole dish in a large pan filled with enough boiling water to reach halfway up the sides of the dish.

Bake until pudding is just set, about 60 minutes.

NOTE: You will need a pan larger than the 2-quart casserole dish. This will act as a double boiler in the oven.

PER SERVING: 76 calories; 4 g fat (43.6% calories from fat); 4 g protein; 6 g carbohydrate; trace dietary fiber; 61 mg cholesterol; 175 mg sodium. Exchanges: 0 grain (starch); 0 lean meat; 0 nonfat milk; ½ fat.

Gorgonzola and Chive Potato Salad

Red bliss potatoes tossed with gorgonzola, sour cream, and red onions

SERVINGS: 16

8 cups red potatoes, *unpeeled and cut into large cubes*
3 tablespoons salt
½ cup red onion, *diced small*
½ cup celery, *diced small*
¼ cup fresh chives, *chopped*
½ cup light sour cream
⅓ cup light mayonnaise
1½ teaspoons cider vinegar
4 ounces gorgonzola cheese
salt and pepper, *to taste*

SERVING IDEAS:
Garnish with crisp bacon crumbles and chives.

Place potatoes in a large pot, add 3 tablespoons of salt, cover with water, and bring to a boil.

Cook 15 minutes or until tender. Drain, and place in a large bowl.

Add onion, celery, and chives; toss gently.

Combine sour cream and next 3 ingredients; stir well.

Stir in cheese.

Pour over potato mixture while still warm; toss gently to coat.

Cover and chill.

PER SERVING: 104 calories; 3 g fat (27.5% calories from fat); 4 g protein; 16 g carbohydrate; 1 g dietary fiber; 9 mg cholesterol; 1,336 mg sodium. Exchanges: 1 grain (starch); ½ lean meat; 0 vegetable; ½ fat; 0 other carbohydrates.

Hazelnut Pilaf

Rice with hazelnuts, mushrooms and cheese

SERVINGS: 8

¾ cup rice, *uncooked*
½ cup hazelnuts, *dry-roasted, chopped*
¾ cup grated cheddar cheese
½ cup onion, *diced*
1 8-ounce can sliced mushrooms, *drained (save liquid)*
1½ cups chicken broth

SERVING IDEA:
Garnish with fresh grated cheddar cheese.

Combine rice, hazelnuts, cheese, onion and mushrooms; place in a greased 1-quart casserole.

Mix mushroom liquid and chicken broth; heat to boiling, and pour over rice mixture.

Cover and bake for 30 to 45 minutes at 350°F. Fluff with fork before serving.

PER SERVING: 159 calories; 7 g fat (40.0% calories from fat); 6 g protein; 18 g carbohydrate; 1 g dietary fiber; 2 mg cholesterol; 211 mg sodium. Exchanges: 1 grain (starch); ½ lean meat; ½ vegetable; 1 fat.

Home-style Green Beans

Fresh green beans simmered with bacon and garlic

SERVINGS: 6

>1½ pounds green beans, *cleaned and ends removed*
>¼ pound bacon, *chopped*
>1 large onion, *chopped*
>2 teaspoons garlic
>¼ cup fresh dill, *chopped*
>1 teaspoon salt
>1 teaspoon pepper

SERVING IDEA:
Serve with
grilled pork chops.

In a medium pot over medium-high heat, sauté bacon until it is well done.
Do not drain fat.

Add onion and garlic to pan, and sauté for 3 minutes.

Next, add green beans, dill, salt and pepper to pot, and fill pot with just enough water
to cover the beans.

Bring to a simmer. Simmer on low for 30 minutes or until beans become soft.

PER SERVING: 40 calories; trace fat (3.0% calories from fat); 2 g protein; 9 g carbohydrate; 4 g dietary
fiber; 0 mg cholesterol; 362 mg sodium. Exchanges: 0 grain (starch); 1½ vegetable; 0 fat.

Honey-Garlic Asparagus

Fresh steamed asparagus with a honey and garlic sauce

SERVINGS: 4

1 pound asparagus
¼ cup Dijon mustard
¼ cup white wine
3 tablespoons honey
½ teaspoon garlic, *minced*
¼ teaspoon fresh thyme, *chopped*
¼ teaspoon pepper
¼ teaspoon salt

SERVING IDEAS:
Garnish with fresh orange slices and chopped parsley.

Add asparagus to boiling, salted water, and cook, covered, about 2 minutes or until barely tender. Drain.

Combine mustard, white wine, honey, garlic, thyme, pepper and salt; mix well.

Pour over cooked asparagus.

PER SERVING: 84 calories; 1 g fat (8.3% calories from fat); 2 g protein; 17 g carbohydrate; 2 g dietary fiber; 0 mg cholesterol; 324 mg sodium. Exchanges: 0 grain (starch); 0 lean meat; ½ vegetable; 0 fat; 1 other carbohydrates.

Mashed Sweet Potatoes

Mashed sweet potatoes with a hint of spice and walnuts

SERVINGS: 8

4 medium sweet potatoes, *peeled and cubed*
2 tablespoons butter
¼ cup skim milk
1 teaspoon allspice
⅔ cup Splenda

SERVING IDEAS:
Garnish with chopped walnuts, and serve with grilled turkey breast.

Boil potatoes until soft.

Remove potatoes from pan, and place in a bowl.

Mash potatoes with potato masher or mixer.

Add butter and milk; stir.

Add Splenda and allspice; stir.

PER SERVING: 93 calories; 3 g fat (28.3% calories from fat); 1 g protein; 16 g carbohydrate; 2 g dietary fiber; 8 mg cholesterol; 42 mg sodium. Exchanges: 1 grain (starch); 0 lean meat; 0 nonfat milk; ½ fat.

Rosemary Roasted Potatoes

Red potatoes roasted with rosemary

SERVINGS: 12

4 pounds red potatoes, *cut in 2-inch pieces*
2 tablespoons olive oil
2 tablespoons fresh rosemary, *chopped fine*
1 tablespoon fresh thyme, *chopped fine*
2 tablespoons fresh garlic, *minced*
2 teaspoons paprika
salt and pepper, *to taste*

SERVING IDEA:
Great with herbed roasted tenderloin.

Preheat oven to 375°F.

Place all ingredients in a large mixing bowl, and mix well. Next, place mixed potatoes into a large roasting pan.

Place potatoes in oven, and roast uncovered for 45 minutes or until tender, turning every 15 minutes to brown evenly on all sides.

PER SERVING: 143 calories; 2 g fat (15.1% calories from fat); 3 g protein; 28 g carbohydrate; 3 g dietary fiber; 0 mg cholesterol; 10 mg sodium. Exchanges: 1½ grain(starch); 0 lean meat; 0 vegetable; ½ fat.

Saffron-Basil Basmati Rice

Basmati rice with fresh basil, tomatoes and garlic

SERVINGS: 8

2 cups basmati rice
½ stick butter
1 bunch fresh basil, *chopped*
2 large plum tomatoes, *chopped*
½ cup scallions, *chopped*
1 teaspoon garlic, *chopped*
8 saffron threads
4½ cups chicken stock

SERVING IDEAS:
Garnish with chopped scallions and fresh chopped tomato.

In a medium sauce pan over medium-high heat, melt butter. Add rice, garlic, tomatoes, scallions, saffron and fresh basil. Sauté in butter for 2 minutes.

Next, add chicken stock. Stir rice with liquid until it comes to a boil. Reduce to a light simmer and cover.

Let cook for 35 minutes over medium-high heat.

Serve.

PER SERVING: 230 calories; 7 g fat (28.3% calories from fat); 5 g protein; 35 g carbohydrate; trace dietary fiber; 16 mg cholesterol; 1302 mg sodium. Exchanges: 2 grain (starch); 0 vegetable; 1 fat.

Southwestern Chive and Corn-Studded Mashed Potatoes

Potatoes mashed with garlic and fresh corn

SERVINGS: 12

3 pounds potatoes, *peeled and chopped*
1 tablespoon olive oil
3 ears fresh corn, *stripped*
2 cloves garlic, *chopped*
2 cups skim milk, *heated*
1 bunch chives, *snipped*
1 tablespoon horseradish
salt and pepper, *to taste*

SERVING IDEAS:
Garnish with corn kernels and chives.

Cook peeled and chopped potatoes in salted water.

Strip the ears of fresh corn, and sauté corn kernels and garlic in the olive oil.

In a mixing bowl, place potatoes and heated skim milk. Mash, and add corn and garlic mixture.

Finish with snipped chives, salt, pepper, and horseradish.

Serve.

PER SERVING: 135 calories; 2 g fat (10.1% calories from fat); 5 g protein; 27 g carbohydrate; 2 g dietary fiber; 1 mg cholesterol; 33 mg sodium. Exchanges: 1½ grain (starch); 0 vegetable; 0 nonfat milk; 0 fat; 0 other carbohydrates.

Spanish Potatoes

Potatoes with bacon, tomatoes, and olives

SERVINGS: 8

1 pound potatoes, *cubed*
2 ounces bacon, *chopped fine*
½ cup sweet peppers, *chopped*
1 large tomato, *chopped*
¼ cup green olives, *quartered*
1 small onion, *sliced*
2 cloves garlic, *chopped*
1 teaspoon chili powder
¾ cup chicken stock
1 tablespoon capers
salt and pepper, *to taste*

SERVING IDEA:
Garnish with fresh chopped cilantro.

In a large sauté pan, cook bacon until well done and crisp.

Drain fat from pan, and add peppers; sauté for 2 minutes.

Next, add tomatoes, olives, onions, garlic, chili powder, potatoes and chicken stock.

Bring to a boil, and let simmer for 15 minutes or until potatoes are soft. Stir in capers.

Let stand for 5 minutes to allow liquids to absorb.

Add salt and pepper to taste.

Serve.

PER SERVING: 106 calories; 4 g fat (34.9% calories from fat); 4 g protein; 13 g carbohydrate; 2 g dietary fiber; 6 mg cholesterol; 370 mg sodium. Exchanges: ½ grain (starch); ¼ lean meat; ½ vegetable; 0 fruit; ½ fat; 0 other carbohydrates.

Stuffed Acorn Squash

Squash stuffed with apples and brown rice

SERVINGS: 4

2 acorn squash, *halved and seeded*
2 tablespoons butter, *melted*
¼ teaspoon salt
¼ teaspoon ground cinnamon
2 cups brown rice, *cooked in chicken broth*
1 cup unsweetened applesauce
½ cup celery, *chopped*
¼ cup toasted pecans, *chopped*
¼ cup Splenda
½ teaspoon onion powder
½ teaspoon ground ginger

SERVING IDEA:
Great with poached or grilled salmon.

Place squash cut side down in a shallow baking pan.

Bake at 350°F for 30 minutes.

Turn squash cut side up; brush with butter. Sprinkle with salt and cinnamon.

Combine rice, applesauce, celery, pecans, Splenda, onion powder and ginger. Fill squash evenly with rice (like a stuffing). Bake uncovered for 20 to 30 minutes.

Serve.

PER SERVING: 288 calories; 8 g fat (22.3% calories from fat); 5 g protein; 55 g carbohydrate; 7 g dietary fiber; 5 mg cholesterol; 175 mg sodium. Exchanges: 3 grain (starch); 0 lean meat; 0 vegetable; ½ fruit; 1½ fat.

Stuffed Tomatoes

Tomatoes stuffed with cheese and herbs

SERVINGS: 8

3 large ripe tomatoes
2 teaspoons salt, *approximately*
2 large cloves garlic, *chopped fine*
¼ cup green onions, *chopped fine*
1 teaspoon fresh thyme, *chopped*
½ teaspoon salt
1 tablespoon fresh basil, *chopped*
½ teaspoon pepper
½ cup Parmesan cheese, *grated*
1 tablespoon olive oil

Cut the tomatoes in half; seed, and press out the juices, but do not mash.

Sprinkle the halves with salt, then turn upside down on a wire cooling rack, and let drain for 10 minutes.

Combine the rest of the ingredients, except the oil, to make the stuffing.

Fill the tomato halves with stuffing, and sprinkle with olive oil. Place in a prepared baking dish.

Bake at 400°F for about 10 minutes or until the tops are browned, but make sure tomatoes are not too soft.

PER SERVING: 50 calories, 1 g fat (57.8% calories from fat); 3 g protein; 3 g carbohydrate, 1 g dietary fiber; 4 mg cholesterol; 764 mg sodium. Exchanges. 0 grain (starch); ½ lean meat; ½ vegetable; ⅓ fat.

Vegetable Medley

Seasonal vegetables seasoned and sautéed

SERVINGS: 8

2 cups baby carrots
2 cups broccoli florets
2 cups asparagus tips
1 large red bell pepper, *julienned*
1 large yellow bell pepper, *julienned*
1 large yellow squash, *sliced ½ inch thick*
1 large zucchini, *sliced ½ inch thick*
1 large onion, *sliced*
¼ cup olive oil
2 cloves fresh garlic, *chopped*
¼ cup fresh lemon juice
salt and pepper, *to taste*

SERVING IDEAS:
Can be served with any of your favorite grain entrées.

In a large sauté pan, heat olive oil.

Add garlic, and sauté until brown.

Next, add vegetables, and sauté on medium-high heat until they are tender.

Add lemon juice, and sauté for 2 minutes. Salt and pepper to taste.

Serve.

NOTE: Cut vegetables the same size so they will cook evenly.

PER SERVING: 118 calories; 7 g fat (51.8% calories from fat); 3 g protein; 13 g carbohydrate; 4 g dietary fiber; 0 mg cholesterol; 29 mg sodium. Exchanges: 2½ vegetable; 0 fruit; 1½ fat.

VEGETARIAN

*I am not a vegetarian because
I love animals; I am a vegetarian
because I hate plants.*

—A. Whitney Brown

Almond Milk

SERVINGS: 4

> 1 cup almonds, *soaked*
> 3 cups water, *filtered*

Place all ingredients in a blender. Blend until almonds are a pulp. Strain through a strainer. Use pulp in a salad.

NOTE: To make seed milks, do as above, but use seeds instead.

PER SERVING: 209 calories; 19 g fat (74.4% calories from fat); 7 g protein; 7 g carbohydrate; 4 g dietary fiber; 0 mg cholesterol; 9 mg sodium. Exchanges: ½ grain (starch); 1 lean meat; 3 fat.

Arame Salad

A perfect seaweed salad with plenty of taste

SERVINGS: 6

8 ounces arame, *soaked and drained*
1 large red onion, *sliced ⅛-inch thick*
1 medium cucumber, *diced fine*
1 large red pepper, *diced fine*
1 medium carrot, *shredded*
¼ cup lemon juice
½ bunch cilantro, *chopped*

Combine ingredients in a large mixing bowl.

Toss. Serve.

SERVING IDEA:
Garnish with
fresh sliced lemon.

PER SERVING: 30 calories; trace fat (4.5% calories from fat); 1 g protein; 7 g carbohydrate; 2 g dietary fiber; 0 mg cholesterol; 7 mg sodium. Exchanges: 0 grain (starch); 0 lean meat; 1 vegetable; 0 fruit.

Asian Salad

Bok choy and bell peppers tossed with sesame oil and lemon

SERVINGS: 10

2 large carrots, *sliced ¼ inch thick*
1 stalk celery, *sliced diagonally*
1 red bell pepper, *julienned*
1 head bok choy, *shredded*
¼ cup sesame seeds
2 teaspoons sesame oil
¼ cup Bragg seasoning mix
¼ cup lemon juice

SERVING IDEA:
Garnish with sesame seeds.

Combine all vegetables in a large mixing bowl. In a blender blend sesame oil, Bragg seasoning mix and lemon juice.

Pour over vegetables, and mix well. Garnish with seeds.

PER SERVING: 41 calories; 3 g fat (55.7% calories from fat); 1 g protein; 4 g carbohydrate; 1 g dietary fiber; 0 mg cholesterol; 14 mg sodium. Exchanges: 0 grain (starch); 0 lean meat; ½ vegetable; 0 fruit; ½ fat.

Avocado Roll-Ups

SERVINGS: 2

1 avocado, *peeled and julienned*
2 tortillas, *spelt*
¼ cup alfalfa sprouts, *rinsed and drained*
¼ cup mung bean sprouts, *rinsed and drained*
¼ cup clover sprouts, *rinsed and drained*
1 small red pepper, *julienned*
1 small sweet potato, *peeled*

Place spelt tortilla on a flat surface. Next, fill with ingredients. Lastly, roll up. Cut in half. Eat.

NOTE: These roll-ups taste great dipped in Tahini dip.

PER SERVING: 251 calories; 16 g fat (52.5% calories from fat); 4 g protein; 28 g carbohydrate; 6 g dietary fiber; 0 mg cholesterol; 21 mg sodium. Exchanges: 1 grain (starch); 0 lean meat; 1 vegetable; ½ fruit; 3 fat.

Beets and Mint

SERVINGS: 6

> 4 medium beets, *shredded*
> ½ bunch mint, *finely chopped*
> ¼ cup fresh-squeezed lemon juice

Combine all ingredients in medium bowl.

Toss. Serve.

PER SERVING: 26 calories; trace fat (2.8% calories from fat); 1 g protein; 6 g carbohydrate; 2 g dietary fiber; 0 mg cholesterol; 43 mg sodium. Exchanges: 1 vegetable; 0 fruit.

Cold Avocado Soup

Avocados blended with veggie juices for a perfect soup

SERVINGS: 10

3 avocados, *cut in halves*
1 cup celery juice
1 cup cucumber juice
1 small red pepper, *diced fine*
1 small white onion, *diced fine*
1 teaspoon cumin
1 teaspoon chili powder
¼ bunch cilantro, *diced fine*
¼ cup fresh lemon juice

SERVING IDEA:
Garnish with chopped red pepper.

Peel and seed avocados. Next, place in blender. Add remaining ingredients. Blend until smooth. Chill and serve.

NOTES: Add Bragg seasoning mix to taste.

PER SERVING: 111 calories; 9 g fat (69.1% calories from fat); 2 g protein; 8 g carbohydrate; 2 g dietary fiber; 0 mg cholesterol; 32 mg sodium. Exchanges: 0 grain (starch); 0 lean meat; ½ vegetable; ½ fruit; 2 fat.

Cold Cantaloupe Soup

Cantaloupe pureed with cinnamon and nutmeg

SERVINGS: 6

    3 cantaloupe, *peeled and seeded*
    1 teaspoon cinnamon
    ½ teaspoon nutmeg
    1 pinch clove
    ½ teaspoon stevia

SERVING IDEA:
Garnish with cinnamon.

Combine all ingredients in a food processor. Puree until liquid. Refrigerate for 1 hour.

Serve.

PER SERVING: 99 calories; 1 g fat (6.9% calories from fat); 2 g protein; 23 g carbohydrate; 2 g dietary fiber; 0 mg cholesterol; 25 mg sodium. Exchanges: 0 grain (starch); 1½ fruit; 0 fat.

Collard Green Salad with Walnuts

Fresh collards and walnuts tossed with bell peppers

SERVINGS: 12

6 cups collard greens, *chopped*
1 medium yellow bell pepper, *diced fine*
1 medium red bell pepper, *diced fine*
1 cup walnuts, *chopped*
1 tablespoon Bragg seasoning mix
¼ cup lemon juice

Combine all ingredients in a bowl. Mix well. Serve.

PER SERVING: 75 calories; 6 g fat (65.4% calories from fat); 3 g protein; 4 g carbohydrate; 1 g dietary fiber; 0 mg cholesterol; 4 mg sodium. Exchanges: 0 grain (starch); ½ lean meat; ½ vegetable; 0 fruit; 1 fat.

SERVING IDEA:
Garnish with fresh chopped scallions.

Creamy Broccoli

Broccoli tossed with tahini, garlic and onion

SERVINGS: 10

1 bunch broccoli florets
1 medium red pepper, *diced*
1 small onion, *diced fine*
1 medium carrot, *shredded*
¼ cup tahini
2 tablespoons lemon juice
1 tablespoon Bragg seasoning mix
2 cloves garlic, *minced*

SERVING IDEA:
Garnish with roasted sesame seeds.

Place all ingredients in a bowl, and mix well. Serve chilled.

PER SERVING: 48 calories; 3 g fat (56.3% calories from fat); 1 g protein; 4 g carbohydrate; 1 g dietary fiber; 0 mg cholesterol; 11 mg sodium. Exchanges: 0 grain (starch); 0 lean meat; ½ vegetable; 0 fruit; ½ fat.

Fennel Salad

*Fennel gives a unique liquorish flavor to this salad
of peppers and onions.*

SERVINGS: 8

3 fennel bulbs, *sliced paper thin*
1 small red onion, *sliced ⅛ inch thick*
1 small red pepper, *julienned*
¼ cup fresh lemon juice
½ bunch parsley, *chopped fine*
1 pinch cardamom

Combine all ingredients in a medium-size bowl. Toss. Serve.

NOTES: This salad tastes better when it sits for 1 hour before serving.

PER SERVING: 42 calories; trace fat (4.8% calories from fat); 2 g protein; 10 g carbohydrate; 4 g dietary fiber; 0 mg cholesterol; 49 mg sodium. Exchanges: ½ grain (starch); ½ vegetable; 0 fruit; 0 fat.

Fresh Veggie and Basil Stir-Fry

Veggies, basil, garlic and whole-wheat pasta

SERVINGS: 8

½ pound whole-wheat pasta, *cooked and drained*
2 tablespoons olive oil
½ cup onion, *diced*
2 cloves garlic, *chopped*
½ cup asparagus tips
½ cup cherry tomatoes, *cut in half*
½ cup yellow squash, *chopped*
½ cup mushrooms, *sliced*
½ cup pea pods, *cut in half*
1 bunch basil, *chopped*
1 teaspoon thyme
salt and pepper, *to taste*

Place all vegetables and spices in a large mixing bowl, and mix well.

Next, heat olive oil in a large sauté pan.

Once olive oil is hot, add vegetables, and cook for 6 minutes.

Add pasta, and sauté for another 2 minutes. Serve.

PER SERVING: 144 calories; 4 g fat (23.0% calories from fat); 5 g protein; 24 g carbohydrate; 3 g dietary fiber; 0 mg cholesterol; 5 mg sodium. Exchanges: 1½ grain (starch); ½ vegetable; ½ fat.

Greek Bean Salad

Three-bean salad with olives and lemon juice

SERVINGS: 4

1 can garbanzo beans, *drained and rinsed*
1 can kidney beans, *drained and rinsed*
1 can black beans, *drained and rinsed*
½ small onion, *chopped fine*
1 cup green olives, *sliced thin*
1 can mushrooms
½ bunch fresh dill, *chopped fine*
3 cloves garlic, *minced*
2 tablespoons olive oil
2 large lemons, *juiced*
salt and pepper, *to taste*

Place all ingredients in a large mixing bowl, and mix well. The salad tastes best if marinated overnight.

PER SERVING: 246 calories; 6 g fat (20.4% calories from fat); 13 g protein; 38 g carbohydrate; 12 g dietary fiber; 0 mg cholesterol; 129 mg sodium. Exchanges: 2½ grain (starch); ½ lean meat; 0 vegetable; 0 fruit; 1 fat.

SERVING IDEA:
Serve with sliced grilled shrimp on top.

Green Bean Salad

Fresh raw green beans tossed with cabbage, garlic and olive oil

SERVINGS: 6

1 pound green beans, *snapped*
1 clove garlic, *minced*
1 medium parsnip, *diced*
1 small onion, *diced*
1 cup red cabbage, *diced*
1 large yellow squash, *diced*
½ cup olive oil
½ teaspoon cayenne
2 tablespoons fresh dill
salt and pepper, *to taste*

SERVING IDEA:
Garnish with fresh chopped scallions.

Place all ingredients in a bowl. Mix. Serve chilled.

PER SERVING: 225 calories; 18 g fat (70.2% calories from fat); 2 g protein; 15 g carbohydrate; 5 g dietary fiber; 0 mg cholesterol; 11 mg sodium. Exchanges: ½ grain (starch); 1½ vegetable; 3½ fat.

Jerusalem Artichoke Fiesta Salad

Artichokes tossed with peppers, garlic, lemon juice and red cabbage

SERVINGS: 6

6 Jerusalem artichokes, *peeled and julienned*
1 small yellow pepper, *diced small*
1 small red pepper, *diced small*
1 small carrot, *diced small*
¼ head red cabbage, *diced small*
¼ cup fresh lemon juice
½ bunch parsley, *diced fine*
1 teaspoon pizza seasoning
1 clove garlic, *minced*
2 tablespoons olive oil

SERVING IDEA:
Garnish with shredded carrots.

Place all ingredients in a medium mixing bowl. Toss. Chill and serve.

NOTES: Add Bragg seasoning mix to taste.

PER SERVING: 132 calories; 3 g fat (22.9% calories from fat); 3 g protein; 24 g carbohydrate; 3 g dietary fiber; 0 mg cholesterol; 11 mg sodium. Exchanges: 4 vegetable; 0 fruit; ½ fat.

Marinated Zucchini

Fresh zucchini topped with Italian dressing

SERVINGS: 10

¼ cup extra-virgin olive oil
¼ teaspoon dried oregano
¼ teaspoon dried thyme
¼ teaspoon dried basil
2 tablespoons fresh lemon juice
2 tablespoons Bragg seasoning mix
3 large zucchini, *sliced*

SERVING IDEA:
Garnish with diced red pepper.

In a blender, blend all ingredients except zucchini. Pour dressing over zucchini. Toss.

Place zucchini in dehydrator trays, and dehydrate for 2 hours at 110°F for 2 hours.

Place on tray, and serve.

PER SERVING: 57 calories; 5 g fat (81.8% calories from fat); 1 g protein; 2 g carbohydrate; 1 g dietary fiber; 0 mg cholesterol; 2 mg sodium. Exchanges: 0 grain (starch); ½ vegetable; 0 fruit; 1 fat.

Mediterranean Salad

Squash, chives and carrots tossed
with a lemon and cayenne-pepper dressing.

SERVINGS: 10

1 large carrot, *julienned*
2 large zucchini, *julienned*
3 large yellow squash, *julienned*
1 bunch chives, *diced fine*
1 bunch oregano, *diced fine*

SERVING IDEA:
Garnish with fresh
grape tomatoes.

Dressing for salad

3 tablespoons extra-virgin olive oil
1 tablespoon fresh lemon juice
¼ tablespoon cayenne pepper

Mix all salad ingredients in a medium mixing bowl.

Combine all dressing ingredients in a blender, and blend.

Combine dressing and salad mixture together. Toss. Serve.

PER SERVING: 49 calories; 4 g fat (73.2% calories from fat); 1 g protein; 3 g carbohydrate; 1 g dietary
fiber; 0 mg cholesterol; 4 mg sodium. Exchanges: 0 grain (starch); ½ vegetable; 0 fruit;
1 fat.

Millet Nori Rolls

SERVINGS: 4

½ cup millet, *cooked*
4 sheets nori
1 small cucumber, *cut into strips*
1 small carrot, *julienned*
1 small red pepper, *julienned*
½ cup alfalfa sprouts

Cook millet, and let it cool.

Once millet is cooled, spread across half of each nori sheet.

Place cucumber, carrot, red pepper and alfalfa sprouts across nori sheets on top of millet.

Roll nori sheets. Cut each nori sheet into five pieces. Serve.

PER SERVING: 121 calories; 1 g fat (9.2% calories from fat); 4 g protein; 24 g carbohydrate; 4 g dietary fiber; 0 mg cholesterol; 10 mg sodium. Exchanges: 1 grain (starch); 0 lean meat; 1 vegetable; 0 fat.

Nut Pâté

SERVINGS: 15

    5 cups pecans, *chopped*
    2 red peppers, *chopped*
    1 stalk celery, *chopped*
    1 bunch parsley, *chopped*
    1 medium onion, *chopped*
    3 medium carrots, *chopped*
    ¼ cup lemon juice
    ¼ cup Bragg seasoning mix

Combine all ingredients in a bowl. Mix with a spoon.

Place ingredients through a juicer (use blank cartridge).

Mold into shape. Serve.

PER SERVING: 256 calories; 24 g fat (80.1% calories from fat); 3 g protein; 10 g carbohydrate; 4 g dietary fiber; 0 mg cholesterol; 11 mg sodium. Exchanges: ½ grain (starch); 0 lean meat; ½ vegetable; 0 fruit; 4½ fat.

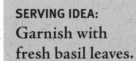

Pesto Soup

*Basil blended with pecans, onion, celery and spinach
to make the perfect soup*

SERVINGS: 8

2 tablespoons olive oil
1 bunch spinach
1 bunch fresh basil
½ cup pecan halves
9 cloves garlic
2 medium carrot, *sliced ½ inch thick*
4 sticks celery, *sliced ½ inch thick*
1 large onion, *julienned*
1 medium red pepper, *julienned*
½ gallon pure water

SERVING IDEA:
**Garnish with
fresh basil leaves.**

Place first five ingredients in a food processor. Process until pesto is thick like paste.

Next, heat water, and then add vegetables and pesto to water. Bring to a simmer.

Soup is done when vegetables are to your desired doneness.

PER SERVING: 81 calories; 6 g fat (67.6% calories from fat); 1 g protein; 6 g carbohydrate; 2 g dietary
fiber; 0 mg cholesterol; 28 mg sodium. Exchanges: 0 grain (starch); 0 lean meat;
1 vegetable; 1 fat.

Pumpkin Seed Cheese

SERVINGS: 6

> 2 cups pumpkin seeds, *roasted, soaked overnight*
> 2 medium cucumbers, *diced*
> ½ cup pignolia, *soaked overnight*
> 1 bunch basil, *fresh picked*

Place cucumbers in a blender. Blend until smooth.

Next, add seeds, nuts, and basil to blender. Blend until smooth (a little water may be added if too thick).

Place in sprouting bag, and drain liquid from seed cheese until desired thickness is achieved.

Serve.

NOTE: Add Bragg seasoning mix to taste.

PER SERVING: 175 calories; 10 g fat (48.8% calories from fat); 7 g protein; 16 g carbohydrate; 5 g dietary fiber; 0 mg cholesterol; 7 mg sodium. Exchanges: 1 grain (starch); ½ lean meat; ½ vegetable; 1½ fat.

Raspberry Mousse

SERVINGS: 6

3 cups fresh raspberries, *rinsed and drained*
½ cup water
2 teaspoons agar
1 tablespoon stevia

Mix water and agar together. Bring to a simmer, and stir until agar is dissolved.

Place in a blender. Add remaining ingredients. Blend until smooth.

Refrigerate until firm.

Blend in blender again until mousse is airy.

Serve.

PER SERVING: 31 calories; trace fat (8.7% calories from fat); 1 g protein; 7 g carbohydrate; 4 g dietary fiber; 0 mg cholesterol; 1 mg sodium. Exchanges: 0 vegetable; ½ fruit.

Red Cabbage Sauerkraut

SERVINGS: 12

> 4 large red cabbage, *shredded*
> 1 large apple, *sliced*

Place half of the red cabbage and in a medium bowl. Pack red cabbage down with hands.

Next, place sliced apples on top of pressed cabbage. Place second layer of cabbage on top of apples, and pack down with hands.

Cover bowl with plastic bag. Place a gallon jug of water on top of plastic bag to keep cabbage packed.

Place in a cool room unrefrigerated for 2 to 3 days (until fermented).

Remove from bowl, and keep refrigerated.

PER SERVING: 15 calories; trace fat (6.2% calories from fat); trace protein; 4 g carbohydrate; 1 g dietary fiber; 0 mg cholesterol; 3 mg sodium. Exchanges: ½ vegetable; 0 fruit.

Sautéed Greens

Collard sautéed with butter and garlic

SERVINGS: 10

3 pounds collard greens (spinach can also be used), *chopped*
2 tablespoons butter
1 small onion, *julienned*
2 tablespoons garlic, *chopped*
1½ teaspoons salt

SERVING IDEAS:
Great with baked
fish or chicken.

Trim the stems from the greens. Soak in lots of cool water to wash away the sand. Shake the water from the greens, and dry them. They must be totally dry before they are cooked.

Place butter in a wide and heavy sauté pan. Add garlic and onion to the pan. Stir, then immediately add greens (all at once if possible).

Stir continuously for about 5 minutes (or until desired doneness). Season with salt, and serve.

PER SERVING: 68 calories; 3 g fat (33.7% calories from fat); 4 g protein; 9 g carbohydrate; 5 g dietary fiber; 6 mg cholesterol; 371 mg sodium. Exchanges: 2 vegetable; ½ fat.

Seed Loaf

SERVINGS: 12

> 2 cups sunflower seeds, *soaked overnight*
> ½ cup pumpkin seeds, *soaked overnight*
> 2 sticks celery, *chopped*
> 1 small carrot, *chopped*
> 1 small white onion, *chopped*
> ¼ bunch fresh basil, *finely chopped*
> ¼ cup fresh lemon juice
> 2 tablespoons Bragg seasoning mix

Combine all ingredients in a medium bowl. Toss.

Put through juicer (use blank cartridge). Form into shape.

Chill and serve.

PER SERVING: 145 calories; 12 g fat (68.6% calories from fat); 6 g protein; 7 g carbohydrate; 3 g dietary fiber; 0 mg cholesterol; 9 mg sodium. Exchanges: ½ grain (starch); ½ lean meat; ½ vegetable; 0 fruit; 2 fat.

Spicy Broccoli with Avocado

Broccoli and avocado tossed with garlic and peppers

SERVINGS: 10

> 2 heads broccoli, *chopped*
> 1 red pepper, *julienned*
> 1 stalk celery, *sliced and salted*
> 2 small red onions, *thinly sliced*
> 1 clove garlic, *minced*
> 1 avocado, *peeled*
> ¼ cup lemon juice
> ¼ cup Bragg seasoning mix

SERVING IDEA:
Garnish with fresh avocados.

Combine all vegetables in a bowl.

Next, combine avocado, garlic, lemon juice, and Bragg seasoning mix in a blender. Blend.

Pour over vegetables. Mix. Serve.

NOTE: Place in a bowl garnished with romaine leaves.

PER SERVING: 78 calories; 4 g fat (34.6% calories from fat); 4 g protein; 11 g carbohydrate; 5 g dietary fiber; 0 mg cholesterol; 39 mg sodium. Exchanges: 1½ vegetable; 0 fruit; ½ fat.

Stuffed Avocados

Avocados filled with spicy corn

SERVINGS: 8

4 avocados, *cut in half*
4 cobs corn, *kernels cut off*
1 medium red pepper, *diced small*
1 small white onion, *diced small*
½ bunch parsley, *chopped fine*
1 teaspoon cumin
1 teaspoon chili powder
¼ cup lemon juice

SERVING IDEA:
Garnish with
fresh lemon slices.

First, cut avocados in half, and place on tray.

Next, cut corn off cobs, and place in a medium mixing bowl.

Add remaining ingredients to corn; mix well.

Fill middle of avocados with corn mixture.

Serve.

PER SERVING: 215 calories; 16 g fat (60.9% calories from fat); 4 g protein; 19 g carbohydrate; 5 g dietary fiber; 0 mg cholesterol; 23 mg sodium. Exchanges: ½ grain (starch); 0 lean meat; ½ vegetable; ½ fruit; 3 fat.

Sweet Potatoes and Parsnips

SERVINGS: 6

> 2 medium sweet potatoes, *julienned*
> 3 large parsnips, *julienned*
> ¼ cup fresh lime juice
> ½ teaspoon cinnamon
> ¼ teaspoon clove, *ground*
> ½ teaspoon stevia

Place all ingredients in a medium mixing bowl. Toss. Serve.

NOTE: Tastes best chilled.

PER SERVING: 134 calories; 1 g fat (3.2% calories from fat); 2 g protein; 32 g carbohydrate; 7 g dietary fiber; 0 mg cholesterol; 17 mg sodium. Exchanges: 2 grain (starch); 0 fruit; 0 fat.

Tahini Dip

SERVINGS: 6

½ cup tahini
¼ cup fresh lemon juice
4 cloves garlic, *minced*
¼ cup water, *filtered*
salt and pepper, *to taste*

Place all ingredients in a blender. Blend until smooth.

Chill and serve.

PER SERVING: 125 calories; 11 g fat (72.2% calories from fat); 4 g protein; 6 g carbohydrate; 2 g dietary fiber; 0 mg cholesterol; 24 mg sodium. Exchanges: ½ grain (starch); ½ lean meat; 0 vegetable; 0 fruit; 2 fat.

Tempeh Lemon Broil
with Onions

SERVINGS: 6

    6 lemon-flavored tempeh
    4 small white onions, *sliced ¼ inch thick*
    4 cloves garlic, *minced*
    1 tablespoon extra-virgin olive oil

Grill tempeh on both sides until hot. In a sauté pan, sauté onions and garlic in olive oil.

Place sautéed onions over grilled tempeh. Serve.

PER SERVING: 381 calories; 15 g fat (33.4% calories from fat); 32 g protein; 35 g carbohydrate; 1 g dietary fiber; 0 mg cholesterol; 13 mg sodium. Exchanges: 2 grain (starch); 3½ lean meat; 1 vegetable; 1 fat.

Tofu Valencia

Tofu sautéed and cooked to perfection with garlic, mushrooms and white wine

SERVINGS: 8

8 slices tofu (hard), *cut into ½-inch slices*
½ teaspoon salt
½ teaspoon pepper
¼ cup flour (Wondra brand)
¼ cup olive oil
½ cup white wine (use real wine, not cooking wine)
2 tomatoes, *peeled and chopped*
½ cup fresh mushrooms, *sliced*
½ cup scallions, *chopped*
1 clove fresh garlic, *chopped*
½ cup vegetable broth

SERVING IDEA:
Great with whole-wheat pasta.

First, salt and pepper tofu.

Next, lightly coat tofu with flour.

Then, place olive oil in a large sauté pan on medium-high heat.

Once olive oil is heated, add coated tofu, and sauté until tofu is golden brown.

When tofu is browned on both sides, add white wine to deglaze the pan.

Then, add tomatoes, mushrooms, scallions, garlic and vegetable broth to pan.

Let tofu dish simmer for 10 minutes or until tofu is cooked. The broth will become thickened while cooking.

PER SERVING: 65 calories; 5 g fat (72.0% calories from fat); 1 g protein; 1 g carbohydrate; 1 g dietary fiber; trace cholesterol; 283 mg sodium. Exchanges: 0 grain (starch); ½ vegetable; 1 fat.

Vegetable Soup

Carrots, celery, onions, squash, herbs and spices
to form the perfect veggie soup

SERVINGS: 6

2 carrots, *peeled and chopped*
½ stalk celery, *diced*
1 large onion, *diced*
1 yellow squash, *diced fine*
1 zucchini, *diced*
1 clove garlic, *minced*
1 teaspoon dried thyme
1 teaspoon dried basil
1 teaspoon dried oregano
½ bunch parsley
1 tablespoon Bragg seasoning mix
1 pinch cayenne
½ gallon pure water

SERVING IDEA:
Garnish with
fresh parsley.

Place vegetables, spices, and water in a large pot.

Bring soup to a boil, and turn down to a light simmer.

Simmer for 30 minutes or until vegetables are soft.

Serve.

PER SERVING: 31 calories; trace fat (6.8% calories from fat); 1 g protein; 7 g carbohydrate; 2 g dietary fiber; 0 mg cholesterol; 26 mg sodium. Exchanges: 0 grain (starch); 1 vegetable; 0 fat.

White Navy Bean Soup

Navy beans never tasted so good

SERVINGS: 10

    1 pound navy beans, *soaked overnight*
    2 cups white onions, *sliced ½ inch thick*
    1 cup carrot, *sliced into rounds*
    1 cup celery, *diced*
    1 bunch parsley, *diced fine*
    4 cloves garlic, *crushed*
    1 tablespoon dried thyme
    1 tablespoon dried basil
    1 tablespoon dried oregano
    2 bay leaves
    salt and pepper, *to taste*

First, drain water from beans. Next, add fresh filtered water to beans (add enough water to cover beans).

Next, add onions, garlic and all dried herbs. Bring soup to a boil, and turn down to a slow simmer. Once beans are cooked, add remaining ingredients.

Let simmer for 30 additional minutes. Serve hot.

NOTES: Add Bragg seasoning mix to taste. You can use any sprouted beans with this recipe.

PER SERVING: 179 calories; 1 g fat (3.9% calories from fat); 11 g protein; 34 g carbohydrate; 13 g dietary fiber; 0 mg cholesterol; 26 mg sodium. Exchanges: 2 grain (starch); ½ lean meat, 1 vegetable; 0 fat.

Acknowledgments

Special thanks to the following staffs for all their support:

Foundation Surgery *Affiliates*
Foundation Bariatric *Affiliates*
WeightWise Bariatric Program

Additional thanks to the following for contributing
their time and skills to this project:

Gregory F. Walton, MD, FACS
Christina B. Corcoran, MS RD/LD
Somer Thompson

Glossary

Foods

arame. A confetti-sliced sea vegetable. It is dark brown and has a delicate texture and flavor. It is often cooked with other vegetables, used in salads, or added to medicinal preparations and baths.

blue cheese. A semisoft cow's milk cheese characterized by blue veins of mold and a very strong aroma.

Bourguignon. Name applied to dishes containing Burgundy wine and often braised onions and mushrooms.

bruschetta. An Italian food originating in Tuscany, which consists of grilled bread rubbed with garlic and topped with tomatoes, olive oil and spices.

couscous. A type of granular pasta from North Africa, cooked like a grain.

crepe. A thin pancake made with egg batter.

fennel. A crisp, aromatic vegetable with a licorice flavor and celery-like texture. The bulb is delicious raw in salads (and great cooked as well), and the feathery fronds can be used as seasoning. The rounder bulbs seem to be more tender than those that are really flat.

hummus. A thick puree of Middle Eastern origin consisting of mashed chickpeas seasoned with tahini (sesame paste), garlic, lemon juice and various other spices.

Jerusalem artichoke. A flowering plant native to North America whose tuber is used as a root vegetable. Also known as sunroot or sunchoke.

manicotti. Tube-shaped noodles about 4 inches long and 1 inch in diameter. They are available packaged in supermarkets. Manicotti are boiled, then stuffed with a meat or cheese mixture, covered with a sauce, and baked.

tahini. A thick, creamy paste or butter made from ground sesame seeds.

tempeh. A chunky, tender soybean cake, which is a traditional Indonesian food.

tofu. A cake made of bean curd, which is made from the milky liquid extracted from soybeans.

tzatziki. A Greek dip made from cucumber, garlic and yogurt or sour cream.

Dry Cooking Methods

bake. To cook food in an oven by dry heat applied evenly throughout the oven.

grill. To cook food with heat from below.

sauté. To cook food in a preheated pan or griddle with minimum amount of fat.

rotisserie. An appliance on which food is rotated over a source of dry heat.

roast. To cook food in dry heat with the aid of fat.

Moist Cooking Methods

boil. To cook in a liquid at 212°F.

braise. To cook in a closed container with liquid in the oven or on the top of the stove.

broil. To cook food with heat from above.

deep fry. To cook food totally immersed in preheated fat or oil.

pan fry. To cook food partially immersed in preheated fat or oil.

poach. To cook food in a liquid at a temperature below the boiling point, at approximately 160°F.

stew. To cook small pieces of food in liquid below the simmering point.

Cooking Resources

Cooking Measurements

½ ounce = 1 tablespoon
3 teaspoons = 1 tablespoon
8 ounces = 1 cup
16 ounces = 2 cups = 1 pint
32 ounces = 2 pints = 1 quart
64 ounces = 2 quarts = ½ gallon
128 ounces = 4 quarts = 1 gallon
1 pound = 16 ounces

Liquid measure is different than dry measure, so use the correct measuring device to ensure success in your recipe.

Cooking Temperatures

Beef
145°F or medium rare.
Bacteria in beef are generally destroyed at this temperature. Ground beef, however, should be cooked to 160°F because of the larger surface areas available for bacterial formation.

Poultry
165°F for white meat, 185°F for dark meat. Salmonella is destroyed at 165°F.

Pork
150°F for medium rare. Trichinosis is destroyed at 137°F.

Fish and Seafood
140°F, opaque and flaky.

Cooking Protein

Believe it or not, the way you cook your protein has everything to do with how well you can digest your protein. Your protein should be moist and tender, *not* moist and chewy. To achieve this requires only a few changes in the way you cook. There are many cooking methods, but choosing the right method makes all the difference.

The first method is **sautéing:** to cook food in a preheated pan or griddle with a minimum amount of fat. Never sauté protein that is more than a ½ inch thick because the outside will burn while the middle remains raw. For even greater success, use a meat mallet to pound your protein to ½ inch thick. Not only does this break down the muscle, it also enables you to cook your food in less time.

The second method is to use a **rotisserie:** to cook food in dry heat while the food is rotating. This is a great method for cooking large cuts of meat such as pork loin, beef tenderloin, whole chicken, and turkey and lamb shank. It is also a great way to purchase already prepared food from most grocery chains and some fast-food restaurants.

Convenience alone makes this method stand out. Roasting and grilling are also great cooking methods, but can be more time consuming. I recommend poaching and steaming only for fish, shellfish and seafood.

Seasoning Does Not Mean Oversalting

Protein has little flavor by itself. This means you need to season it. Lightly seasoning your food used to work, but now that you are chewing your food 20 to 30 times per bite, it just isn't enough. You want the first chew to have as much flavor as the last chew. This can be accomplished in several ways. First remember, "fresh is best." Use fresh herbs and spices. Next, make sure your protein is fully coated with the herbs and spices, and yes, use two to three times the amount of seasoning you are used to. Remember, if you use a lot of salt you will become thirsty and not be able to drink for 90 minutes.

Choosing and Preparing Protein
Beef

When choosing beef, there are a few rules you need to follow. You can no longer eat inexpensive cuts of beef. Cheaper cuts of beef such as brisket, bottom or top round, and flank steak have almost no fat marbling, which in turn causes the meat to become very dry when cooking. Great cuts of beef to use are beef tenderloin, rib eye, prime rib, porterhouse, T-bone, and New York strip. The opposite rule is used when purchasing ground beef. You need the least expensive ground chuck. This ground chuck has more fat, which gives the ground meat moisture and flavor.

Beef should not be eaten medium well to well done. When prepared to this degree, all moisture is lost, and beef will become chewy and almost impossible to swallow. When preparing ground chuck, do not overcook. As a rule, cook ground beef until it turns gray. If you cook it further, it will be too dry to digest. Remember, protein has little flavor, so season it well. Also, the best way to prepare beef is using dry heat cooking methods, which are sautéing, cooking on a rotisserie, grilling, baking and roasting. If you choose to stew or braise your meat, you need to use expensive cuts of meat and cook for a long period of time. In most cases it takes up to 8 hours for beef to become tender.

Poultry

Most bariatric patients prefer dark meat because of the moisture content. This does not mean you cannot eat white meat. It just needs to be prepared and cooked differently. When cooking white meat, you should pound the chicken out to ¼ inch thickness, and then place it in a large skillet over medium-high heat. Sauté the poultry for 1½ minutes on each side. If the chicken is not done in 3 minutes, your pan was not hot enough or your chicken was not ¼ inch thick. The number one reason white meat chicken is too dry to eat is because it is overcooked. A rotisserie is another great option for preparing poultry.

Poultry should be cooked to 155°F. Higher temperatures will dry out the poultry. At any lower temperature the poultry will be raw.

Marinating chicken in acidic marinades, such as mojo, will help break down the muscle in chicken while adding flavor. Remember, leftover poultry goes well in cold salads and hot dishes.

Pork, Lamb and Liver

Pork, lamb and liver are also great protein sources. These meats are most tender when cooked in dry heat or sautéed. Pork and lamb are great marinated and can be cut up and stir-fried or placed on skewers and grilled over medium-low heat.

American lamb is not as pungent as New Zealand lamb and has become more popular over the past ten years; it can be found in most supermarkets and restaurants.

Beef and chicken livers are very soft and can be made into fresh liver pâtés. They can also be sautéed on their own and seasoned well to make a great meal. The possibilities are endless with these protein foods. You can always use lamb, liver and pork in any recipes where beef or chicken is used.

Fish and Seafood

Fish is best eaten when fresh. When frozen, fish loses some of its moisture and flavor. Fresh fish should not smell fishy; in fact, it should have almost no smell at all.

Poaching is a quick, healthy way to infuse flavor into the fish while cooking. When poaching, use white wine or fish stock instead of water. Grilling, sautéing, and broiling will also make fish dishes taste great. Remember, use fresh herbs and spices. For great flavor, use butter and olive oil when sautéing and baking.

Most fish can be used the next day for cold salad preparations such as seafood salad with calypso sauce, shrimp salad with dill, and salmon fish dip with capers and fresh lemon juice. The possibilities are limitless.

Index

INDEX

WeightWise
Bariatric Program

WeightWise Bariatric Program is a comprehensive weight management and wellness program developed by Foundation Bariatric *Affiliates*. WeightWise is different from any other program because it is tailored to suit the needs of each individual dealing with weight management. Whether a member's goal can be accomplished through a medical weight management program or through the help of surgery, our physicians, dietitians, exercise physiologists, psychiatrists and support staff are trained to educate him or her through each step of the process.

WeightWise Bariatric Program helps our members achieve their goals and maintain their weight through behavior modification, healthy nutrition, and encouragement to exercise and to stay active. Not only do we strive to meet all of our members' physical needs throughout their journey, but we also work to meet their emotional needs by providing ongoing support groups and counseling. WeightWise HealthPlexes provide our members with access to every component they will need under one roof—from a nutrition store and gym to medical laboratories and offices that provide sleep studies, medical check-ups, nutritional counseling, fitness assessments and meeting spaces.

For members who decide on surgery, Foundation Bariatric Hospitals use state-of-the-art equipment and surgical techniques along with a highly trained, specialized staff that makes our hospitals second to none. Our surgeons use the latest laparoscopic techniques in their weight-loss surgeries because they have proven effective at producing significant and sustained weight loss, along with providing improvements in co-morbid conditions and quality of life, not to mention a shortened recovery time.

For more information about the WeightWise Bariatric Program, visit WeightWise.org or call 1.866.WGTWISE (948-9473). More information about Chef Dave products can be found on the e-Store located on WeightWise.org or by visiting one of the WeightWise HealthPlex nutrition stores.

About the Author

Where do I start? Well, I was born in sunny West Palm Beach, Florida, in 1972, and until the age of six or seven I was always a healthy weight. Sometime after that, I began to pack on the pounds, and my doctors were after me to exercise and eat less. I can only imagine what it would have been like to be a "normal" kid, because I was wearing "HUSKY" clothes and shopping in the men's department by the time I was twelve. I was constantly teased and taunted, and my self-esteem was not the best—not to mention that I looked like a 20-year-old fat man!

While in my teens, I lost about 50 pounds and struggled daily to keep the weight off. Throughout high school I managed to stay right around 230 pounds, which was even more of a struggle. I felt the need to compensate for my weight by always being the 'Jolly Fat Guy,' but inside I really wanted to be the 'Cool Thin Guy,' who could get any girl he fancied, eat whatever he wanted, shop in a normal store, and buy whatever clothes were in style.

At eighteen I found the love of my life, someone who was interested in the real me and could see past my size. After five years of dating, we were married. As most people know, getting married often means allowing oneself to relax, and for me this meant trouble. I went from weighting 245 pounds on my wedding day to weighing over 360 pounds in only five years.

My life, as well as my outlook on life, changed dramatically on August 6, 2000, when my son Noah was born. I realized just how much my size limited what I was able to do. I could not sit on the floor and play with my child. Taking him for an afternoon walk, or any walk for that matter, was almost impossible. I found myself always sitting on the couch, watching him play instead of actually getting down and interacting with him. I regretted that I was unable to play a more active role in his life. That's when I realized I had to have bariatric surgery. I knew that for me the procedure was a life or death situation. I also knew that if I did not take back control of my life, I would not live long enough to see my son graduate or get married, or even get a chance to know my grandchildren.

So after a ton of research and support from my wife, I set out on a new adventure:

reclaiming what was rightfully mine. I was going to get my life back! My surgery date was January 28, 2002. I underwent the laparoscopic procedure and was out of the hospital in only four days. My biggest fear was not the surgery itself but not waking up after the surgery. This faded instantly when I awoke to see my wife at my bedside. I knew my new life was just beginning.

In just the first month I lost 40 pounds and was honestly amazed at my success. I had very little trouble after surgery and am now able to do things that thin people often take for granted: I can fasten my seat belt, go up in my attic, sit in a booth at any restaurant, shop in normal stores, and, most importantly, I can be a father to my two sons.

My work with the WeightWise Bariatric Program of Foundation Bariatric *Affiliates* has led me to Oklahoma, where I now reside with my wife of ten years, Mary, and my two boys, Noah, 6, and Michael, 2.